AT THE ELBOWS OF MY ELDERS

AT THE ELBOWS OF MY ELDERS

One Family's Journey Toward Civil Rights

GAIL MILISSA GRANT

Missouri History Museum
St. Louis
Distributed by the University of Missouri Press

To my father, David Marshall Grant,

who gave me everything

and

To my mother, Mildred Hughes Grant,

who gave me even more

Library of Congress Cataloging-in-Publication Data

Grant, Gail Milissa, 1949-
At the elbows of my elders : one family's journey toward civil rights / Gail Milissa
Grant.
p. cm.
Includes bibliographical references and index.
ISBN 978-1-883982-66-9 (cloth : alk. paper)
1. Grant, Gail Milissa, 1949---Family. 2. African Americans--Missouri--Saint
Louis--Biography. 3. African American families--Missouri--Saint Louis. 4. Saint
Louis (Mo.)--Biography. 5. African Americans--Civil rights--Missouri--Saint
Louis--History--20th century. 6. Civil rights movements--Missouri--Saint Louis-
-History--20th century. 7. Saint Louis (Mo.)--Race relations--History--20th
century. 8. African Americans--Civil rights--History--20th century. 9. Civil
rights movements--United States--History--20th century. 10. United States--Race
relations--History--20th century. I. Title.
F474.S29N435 2008
977.8'6600496073--dc22
2008024219

Distributed by the University of Missouri Press
Printed and bound in the United States by Sheridan Books
Cover and book design by Madonna Gauding

CONTENTS

FOREWORD

"*A*ND THAT'S THE WAY SHE GOES." THUS ENDED MANY of the tales related by Gail Milissa Grant's father. She could never figure out the exact meaning of "this unexplained punctuation mark," but she could always recognize whether it was an expression of irony or resignation or sometimes a straightforward "gotcha!"

Ms. Grant's father was David M. Grant, a St. Louis–born African American who became a prominent attorney and civil rights activist beginning in the 1930s. Yet the stories she heard from her father reach back to even earlier days and, mingled with her mother's memories and what they had both learned from their parents, offer us a picture of St. Louis and a version of life that many of us would otherwise never experience. We are indebted to her for this unusual perspective on the struggle for equal rights and even common courtesy. This is the struggle that every African American individual, family, and community had to face. Black middle-class families, like the Grants, built their own lives and fortunes within the burdens of discrimination and at the same time laid a solid foundation for the officially recognized movement that would burst through in later decades.

We can identify with much of what Grant recounts. My grandmother wasn't an expert embalmer like our author's, but I can relate to the family lore passed down from parent to child. The "mercilessly hot St. Louis summers," family vacations, schools and parties, conflict between family members, pride, ambitions, dreams, and disappointments are common to all of us. Some of us understand through personal experience the cruel prejudices that inflict long-lasting bruises or permanent scars on souls and psyches or, more positively, drive into action the recipients of such ignorant behavior. To those of us whose skin color has allowed us to escape those trials, Grant tells us tales worth pondering.

We have all sat at the "elbows of our elders," but have we all listened with the attention with which Gail Milissa Grant absorbed her family's stories? Her memoir reminds us what a treasure we have in the history of those who have preceded us and urges us to take account and add their narratives to ours. It also cautions us to preserve and share these stories, as our obligation to our ancestors, our descendants, and our community as well.

—Robert R. Archibald, Ph.D.
President, Missouri History Museum

Acknowledgments

*I*STARTED THIS PROJECT IN EARNEST MORE THAN TEN YEARS ago and I have many people to acknowledge for their encouragement along the way.

First off, my thanks go to the men in my life. My husband, Gaetano Castelli, not only continually prodded me to finish the book, he also provided me with the space and freedom to squirrel myself away in my office in Rome and to travel to the United States whenever I wanted to spend time with my mother and conduct research. Above all, he looked at me with pride every time we discussed my work. My brother, David, read and reread my drafts to make sure that I got our father's "voice" just right. Since he is a writer himself, I was humbled by his cogent remarks and constructive advice.

Heartfelt thanks go to the Missouri History Museum for publishing my book and especially to Dr. Robert Archibald for his insightful foreword, and to Victoria Monks and Lauren Mitchell for their guidance.

The following are St. Louis elders whose names I did not include in my book but whom I want to acknowledge for their role in my life and in this story.

Ms. Elner Bolden

Mr. Ray Collier

Mrs. Lucy Collier

Mr. John Cousins

Dr. Benjamin Davis

Mrs. Bessie Draper

The Hon. George Draper

Dr. John Gladney

Mrs. Clarice Gladney

Mrs. Clara Young Gordon

Mr. Donald Gunn, Esq.

Mrs. Dovie Howell

Mrs. Jacquelyn Llewellyn

Mr. Henry McKell

Dr. Helen Nash

Mrs. Ann Davis Pittman

Mrs. Fannie Pitts

Mrs. Ruth Richards

The Hon. Harold Russell

Dr. Sidney E. Smith

Mrs. Weldon "Sugar" Smith

Mrs. Melba Sweets

Mr. Henry Twigg, Esq.

Mrs. Mildred Twigg

Mrs. Doris Weathers

Dr. E. B. Williams

Mr. Harold Young

I could not have finished my manuscript without my "official" readers, June Gordon Dugas, Elaine Walker-Emory, Katherine Inez Lee, Milton Moskowitz, and Joan Westley, who were all eager to read for me and made me feel it was, in no way, an imposition.

Bouquets of flowers go to my coterie of friends who never tired of listening to me talk about my book: Vicki Assevero, June Baldwin, Ruth Cooke-Gibbs, Kathy Davis, Lynne Edwards, Angelique Electra, Ramona Harper, Leonade Jones, David Levering Lewis, Francille Rusan-Wilson, JoDell Shields, Mary Helen Thompson, Scotti Williston, and Colleen Keegan, who urged me just to start writing.

I thank the friends and associates of my parents whom I interviewed: attorneys Margaret Bush-Wilson, George Carper, Forriss Elliott, Frankie Farmer, Ira Young, Mrs. Mildred Roxborough, Dr. Frank Richards, the Hon. James W. Symington, Mrs. Ina Boon, and Mrs. Virgie McNeal. I send prayers of gratitude to those who contributed to my research and passed away during the preparation of the book: Mrs. Leola Amoureaux Duckett and her son, Herbert, Judge Theodore McMillian, and Mr. Benny Rodgers. My cousin Louise Grant Dobson died many years ago, but she left behind her master's thesis on the St. Louis unit of the March on Washington movement that helped me fill in many of the blanks in my father's stories.

My mother was an immensely private person and I must again thank her for opening up to me for this book. "I don't remember much," she would say; "Oh, just make it about your father." Then, fortunately, she would start recounting so much more than what she thought she knew and would refresh my memory of the stories. As Daddy slowed down, my mother, brother, and I encouraged him to write a book. In hindsight, I understand why he wouldn't. He needed to have an audience to regale and laugh along with. When I interviewed him and he relived his valiant efforts to secure civil rights for all, the glow and magic of those times shone brightly. It was inspiring to watch. So, again I thank my father for planting my feet on the ground and my mother for keeping my head in the skies.

INTRODUCTION

AS A CHILD OF THE 1950S IN ST. LOUIS, MISSOURI, I spent a lot of time with my parents and older brother, David, around our dining room table, a large wooden one always dressed with an ironed linen tablecloth and matching napkins. We gathered there mostly to eat the scrumptious meals Mommy prepared with ease. We also huddled to play cards, piece together jigsaw puzzles, master board games, and engage in powwows where we attempted to resolve squabbles that arose each week. This latter activity took the shape of a fairly formal "family council," including minutes of the proceedings, dutifully transcribed and reviewed each time we met. My father's profession as an attorney made this accounting mandatory. The issues were recurring, in large part, and focused on monotonous chores, such as washing the dishes, taking out the trash, and cleaning our rooms. The most heated, and in hindsight the most hilarious, part of these summits centered on "who started it." In other words, we pointlessly tried to sort out who struck the first blow that ignited the quarrels that David and I, in some ways, couldn't get enough of.

However, the highlight of our moments together came when our parents, David and Mildred, began spontaneously talking about their pasts: retelling luscious stories of their youth and coming-of-age tales about college and drawing portraits of their social circle. Yet each account was tainted, almost invariably, by the racism they confronted as African Americans. They usually managed to outwit the culprits and made us laugh out loud at the punch lines. Nonetheless, their encounters, so laced with humor, scarcely disguised the pain they felt or lessened the impact that prejudice had had on their aspirations. Above all, these stories underscored how they and their friends overcame the insults to their humanity, and they helped my brother and me cope with the intolerance we were already facing. We lived in an oasis of sorts, surrounded on all sides by white, blue-collar neighbors who had never seen the likes of us: In the late 1940s, my parents had purchased a house smack-dab in the middle of the largely segregated south side of the city.

Through my father's countless yarns, we learned of an era when riverboats still cruised up and down the Mississippi, carrying travelers who booked passage as much for the entertainment (by Louis Armstrong, for instance) and the scenery as for arrival at their destination. He spoke of similar trips aboard ships that crisscrossed Lake Michigan in the summers, where Bessie Smith headlined the bill. My father witnessed many of these soirées since he was sometimes aboard playing cello in his brother's band or waiting tables fresh out of high school. He talked about how these voyages introduced him to jazz and especially the blues, which became a lasting passion of his. He also worked as a club car porter and even tried his hand at the family profession of chiropody before taking up law at Howard University in Washington, D.C.

My mother described her sheltered upbringing as the only child of some of the first black undertakers in the state of Missouri. She was coddled and cuddled by her parents and their employees, and usually driven to elementary school in the family's limousine—a ritual that made her blanch. She left St. Louis as a preteen to attend a largely Caucasian high school in San Diego, California, and returned to the Midwest as a precocious sixteen-year-old, dashing off to a whirl of parties and balls before moving to Chicago for college. She began visiting St. Louis regularly in the early 1940s to lend her parents a hand with their business, became reacquainted with my father, and married him. She then joined her husband in a movement he had been spearheading for almost fifteen years, teaming up with some of the most famous black people in America for a grueling yet exhilarating war against racism.

It was at the elbows of my elders and their circle that I listened to their tales and traveled into their past with them. I was astounded by their courage and captivated by the alluring, yet divided world they fashioned to buffer themselves from a system of strictly enforced laws and customs, known as Jim Crow laws, which oppressed Negroes.[1] I learned that I was part of the next generation that would benefit from their crusade and that we would be expected to accept their baton, transform it into something even more powerful, and pass it on to those to come. Above all, their dignified example helped me deal with my own feelings when reminded of my second-class citizenship, which came sooner and more often for my brother and me than for most of the children of our parents' friends, who lived in colored neighborhoods on the near north side.

---

[1] In wrestling with what to call Americans of African ancestry in this book (the nomenclature has varied over the centuries and is still evolving), I attempted to use the words commonly employed during the decade or period I am describing. If I deviate from this norm, it is only in the interest of style.

I believe my parents chose to "walk their talk" when they bought a house on St. Louis's forbidding south side in 1947. It was the year before the Supreme Court ruled that restrictive covenants, which were routinely used to prevent Negroes from buying property in white neighborhoods, were unenforceable. I silently wondered why they plopped us into this hostile territory, and years would pass before I fully comprehended my parents' resolve to raise us outside of the more-secluded cocoon available on the "other" side of town. I left St. Louis when I turned twenty-four and wound up traveling throughout the world, interacting with people from all walks of life and readily handling almost any situation I faced, including preparing overseas visits for U.S. presidents. I felt fortified by my parents' refusal to accept limitations and encouraged to step outside of my own comfort zone. And each time I returned to south St. Louis, I witnessed the concrete results of their move. In a locale that was as narrow minded as any in America, I now see a hodgepodge of people of every color, and from every continent, living next to each other in relative peace.

My family is representative of many black, middle-class, and blue-collar people who, beginning at the turn of the twentieth century, went to school, paid their dues, and forced America to face its degrading treatment of Negroes. This overlooked sector took immeasurable chances long before the modern civil rights movement began in the 1950s and became its backbone. They challenged the United States to live up to its ideals and promises before the laws aimed at dismantling racial discrimination were passed. Although the "Negro problem" was blamed implicitly on the victims of it, black people ironically exemplified the classic American success story. Through one exceptional act of courage after the other, they crippled Goliath. By quilting together a series of vignettes that describe their daring, I hope to sketch a picture of what they encountered and, moreover, what I learned from them. Above all, I want to honor these extraordinary, everyday people who set in motion a social movement with neither boundary nor end.

I.

THE MAMMOTH TEARDROP

Life in South St. Louis during the 1950s

*W*HEN I GREW UP IN ST. LOUIS IN THE 1950S, IT WAS A town of contradictions: at once brawny and slumbering, industrial and mom and pop, ethnically diverse and staunchly segregated, corn fed and among the ten largest cities in the United States. It was also known as the American city that typified the most Northern of Southern cities and the most Southern of Northern. St. Louis's own poet Fannie Cook called it "a Northern town with southern exposure." Shaped like a mammoth teardrop, St. Louis was divided in its white and Negro populations between its south and north poles. Some colored people had resided alongside whites on the south side during the nineteenth century, and their children even had attended public and parochial schools with whites.

By the early twentieth century, however, most blacks lived within the northeast quadrant of the city, with a substantial morsel bitten from its center. Not many Negroes dared to board streetcars that ran past Chouteau Avenue, the invisible dividing line between midtown St. Louis and the intimidating south side, although public transportation in St. Louis was never restricted by race. The only exceptions to this unwritten rule were those who lived within the Shaw (midtown) and Carondelet (far south side) neighborhoods. My parents did more than merely travel across this border; in 1947, they decided to live in the south side's bosom. No crosses were burned on our minuscule front lawn, and the residents didn't flee to the suburbs when we arrived. Largely blue-collar folk, some of them were clinging by a hangnail to their own homes, rented or otherwise, and couldn't imagine moving anywhere. By contrast, my father practiced law and was a prominent civil rights leader. "If you can't get Perry Mason, call Attorney Grant," increasingly became a motto for any colored person in a jam. We had the first television set, air conditioner, and garbage disposal on our block, and I got the fanciest hula hoop to wiggle my hips around in. But no amount of money or status could shield us from bigotry.

Before kindergarten, I received the first of many lessons on being colored in the United States from a neighborhood boy, who was even younger than me. When he glimpsed the soles of my feet, he wondered why they were white, then told me to go back to Africa. Although I couldn't handily pinpoint the continent on a map, I had a vague notion that my ancestors were born there. From the Tarzan movies I'd seen, however, as well as an African cannibal who chased the Little Rascals one week on TV, shouting "Yum, yum, eat 'em up!," Africa didn't seem very inviting.

Fortunately, our next-door neighbors presented no major problems. Italian Americans owned a two-family flat that hugged our house to the west. They were friendly from the moment they moved in, and I made my first best friend with their middle daughter, Mary. We even almost shared a birthday. Like most best friends, she and I had our spats. As our rows intensified, we sometimes resorted to flinging racial epithets at each other. "Nigger" packed a bigger punch than "dago" or "wop," so she usually won. I always felt ashamed when I called her a name because my parents warned that it proved nothing and settled even less. But sometimes I couldn't resist. After we dried our eyes and let a few days pass, one of us would end the standoff by calling out across the backyard fence, "Can you come out and play?" and we would be inseparable all over again.

David M., David W., Mildred, and Gail Milissa Grant, ca. 1952.

I knew she didn't mean any real harm, and at times she came to my defense. One day, she, her sister, and I played King of the Hill on their patch of a front yard; a man approached, slowed his pace, and stared me down.

"Are you a nigger?" he asked.

On impulse, she slapped the same question back in his face; he did an abrupt double take before stepping quickly down the sidewalk. At times, Mary withstood another of the era's most insulting labels. I was used to having south siders occasionally yell "nigger" at me as they sped by in their cars. When she was with me, she might get tagged as a "nigger lover" as well.

She and I would roam the nearby blocks together, talking to everyone we met. One time a woman invited us into her living room. She was a widow without children and she wanted to show us her collection of urns, filled with her dogs' ashes and strewn across her mantelpiece. I remember wondering where her husband's ashes were, but they were nowhere in sight. We tried to enliven the summers by putting on plays and skits in my basement or backyard garage and were assured of at least one in the audience. We'd force Mary's little sister to sit and watch as we donned homemade costumes, acted out several parts, and tried to remember our lines.

Mary and her family crowded together on the ground floor in a four-room apartment where I spent many summer afternoons with her and her mother and sister, watching soap operas. Her paternal grandparents lived above them. Her grandfather, who had been a carpenter and always sported starched overalls, never learned English, but his wife spoke it fluently, with only a whisper of an accent.

Our neighbor to the east was, in fact, colored, so technically, we couldn't lay claim to having integrated our neighborhood. But Mrs. Lewis was so light skinned that, as a child, it never occurred to me that she was a Negro. My own mother looked almost white and so did some of her friends who lived on the north side. In spite of their keen features, straight hair, and buttermilk skin, they were all clearly colored women to me. My parents never referred to Mrs. Lewis's race, so I never thought twice about it. I just remember that she draped herself in black, seemed roped to the ground whenever she plodded through her backyard, and never spoke to anyone. Later on, I learned that there were four or five other colored families living within a six-block radius of our house. We were like a few freckles, scattered across an otherwise lily-white face.

When Mrs. Lewis died, another Italian American family bought her house, and they were cordial. My father even nestled the owner in his arms as he died years later from a sudden heart attack; Daddy rushed to his side when he heard his wife come screaming from her house. Yet we rarely, if ever, socialized as families in either of our neighbors' homes or they in ours.

South siders were a motley lot. They included most ethnic groups in America at the time, and each had a distinctive style. The Dutch saw themselves as the epitome of cleanliness, with their frenzied window washing, persistently instructing their neighbors to follow suit. The Irish appeared a bit secretive, and the Italians anything but. Some others, derogatively referred to as "DPs" (displaced persons), were from Eastern Europe and spoke English with thick accents. The Germans opened their own beer hall just east of our house and a bakery to the west, where we were always served in spite of their obvious dislike of Negroes. My father savored greeting the owners with the German phrases he still remembered from elementary school. With mouths agape, they promptly delivered a warm slice of apple strudel or chunk of coffee cake. Although each group maintained some ethnocentricity by what it ate, or where it worshipped, or how it clung to its native tongue, they all seemed bound to one another by the tight rein they held on the neighborhood. Satisfied with their insularity, they wanted their part of town to stay the way it was. The south side was a safe American harbor for them.

Ironically, we colored had reached North American shores long before any of them, yet we were treated like the newcomers. I soon learned that my family could trace its colored lineage back to some of my great-great-grandparents before we dissolved into check marks on census slave records. My father even personally knew one of his great-grandfathers who had come from Tennessee following emancipation. Furthermore, Daddy had female ancestors on his mother's side who had been snatched from Madagascar in the nineteenth century. Part of my family's lore included these two sisters, one of whom was Daddy's great-grandmother. Touted as teenage daughters of a chieftain there, they were reputedly stolen one day as they picked fruit or nuts in an outlying field; by the 1830s, they resided in Adams County, Mississippi. They were described as assertive and confident, so much so that Affie, the eldest, threw boiling water on the white doctor she worked for in Natchez when he insulted her. She escaped to her sister's, my great-great-grandmother, whose name remains a mystery to us. Affie refused to be called an African and, in her own patois, would state firmly, "Me no Africano! Me Malagash!" My father had other relatives, a maternal aunt nicknamed "Mattie" and her husband, who had traveled to South Africa in the early twentieth century as some of the first colored Baptist missionaries in Cape Town. It took me a while to see how firmly American I was, as opposed to my neighbors. As this finally dawned on me, I was astonished by the chutzpah of those so recently native born.

There were no Jews, at least none that I knew of until I entered adulthood and learned that they had owned the few stores we entered comfortably as children. At the neighborhood shoe store, the salesmen measured our feet alongside their white customers', with the aid of a shoe-fitting fluoroscope, a tall, wooden cabinet where we would insert our feet to be x-rayed. We delighted in peering into it and wiggling our skeleton-like toes after they had determined our size. We had our footwear repaired at Sam's, where a white man commonly shined my father's shoes, an ironic role reversal I only came to appreciate fully as an adult. I looked forward to going to these stores because smiling salespeople always warmly greeted us.

Mrs. Mattie Murff, ca. 1920.

Houses on the south side were multistory and made from sharp-edged, red brick. Topped by pitched or level roofs, they had small backyards with narrow gangways that hopscotched between most homes. Some were single-family dwellings, but most were two-family flats, except for on the far south side, where ranch-style homes predominated and sat on broad, manicured lawns. Nearly all of the streets were clean and quiet, and the commercial sections orderly.

Unidentified neighbor, David W. Grant, and Maggie Johnson holding Gail Milissa Grant at the Grant home on Arsenal Street, 1949.

On the face of it, the near north side shared the same architectural ingredients with its southern half, but seemed to be wrapped in gauze, rendering most things a little less sharp. Some streets were a tad scruffy, others broad and direct. There was less open space, and some parts of the north side were unsafe. The more-residential neighborhoods were subdued, but the mercantile districts bustled. Everything looked as if it moved faster there—the cars, the people, and the moments. Amid the fanfare, however, there was a solidarity that oozed from the bricks and bound the community together. North siders knew who they were (Negroes), where they came from (mostly the South), and where they wanted to go (up the American social and economic ladder).

Overall, the two siders, south and north, had only fleeting contact but had explicit opinions about the other. Negroes considered white people deceitful and menacing, and whites saw Negroes as inferior and frightful. Each side would soon be compelled to interact and reassess its opinions. Through the work of colored individuals and communities throughout the United States, court cases were being filed against legal segregation and being won. For instance, in 1954 the Supreme Court ruled that "separate" education for Negroes could never be "equal" schooling and, even earlier (in 1948), outlawed racially restrictive covenants. Although years went by before even partial implementation of these legislative landmarks, America was being redefined. With all of these changes looming over everyone's heads and the outcome far from certain, fear and racial tension branded the 1950s.

While some of our white neighbors grew antagonistic, the colored community from the north side of town posed another challenge. They wondered aloud, "Why do they want to live all the way over there? Who are they trying to be?" In fact, my parents' friends found it so puzzling that they sometimes inserted a meaningful pause before mentioning where we lived: "Did you know that Dave and Mildred live on . . . the south side?"

On the face of it, the reason was simple. As a recently married couple, they had little money. So when a close friend offered to sell them his family home at a bargain-basement price, they grabbed it.

I, too, silently questioned their motives. Although I did not connect all of the dots of their lives until adulthood, I eventually realized that they had mostly lived outside of the mainstream. These patterns, begun in childhood, continued throughout their lives and led them to buy a three-story house at 3309 Arsenal Street and integrate the heart of the very white near south side. Their tales helped me construct a picture of my parents before I knew them.

2.

But Why Do I Have to Ride a Streetcar to School?

Turn-of-the-Century St. Louis

$\mathcal{M}$Y FATHER, DAVID MARSHALL GRANT, WAS BORN ON New Year's Day 1903, on the third floor of a house at 3228 Lawton Avenue where his family lived. His parents had little choice as to where my grandmother would give birth to him and his three older siblings; at that time, St. Louis had no hospital with a colored maternity ward. Shortly thereafter, the Grants moved to the 3500 block of Lawton, three blocks to the west. "Most of my early life was spent between these two houses," my father recalled. "I think we were the first colored family to move onto the 3500 block."

Known as Mill Creek Valley, the entire neighborhood would soon change complexion. In the meantime, however, the Board of Education provided two 2½-cent, paper streetcar tickets on a daily basis to any Negro child who lived near a white school but far from a colored one. As the baby of the family, my father was the last to learn why he and his sister and two brothers had to rise earlier than their neighborhood pals and ride a streetcar to school. Willie, the first-born son, told him that it was because they were colored and white people said they weren't good enough to go to

The Grant children, ca. 1906. Left to right: David M., John, Vivian, and William. Courtesy of Ann Camille Saunders.

school with them. Whenever the subject came up, their mother, Elizabeth Holliday Grant, tried her best to drum this notion out of them. My father said she would tell them that anybody who looks down on another because of something as uncontrollable as skin color needs to be crawling in the dirt with reptiles. "In fact, my mother bred it into us that we were superior to white people. She felt that way because she judged people by what they did and how they treated others, and not by the way they looked. And so should we," he said.

The Grant children grew accustomed to being awakened earlier than others but never fully accepted being sent into the darkness of still winter mornings to ride a streetcar that took them more than two miles away from their home. In ascending order, my father, Johnny, William, and Vivian traveled to the Phyllis Wheatley School, named for the Negro poet from Boston. Carline Elementary stood less than four blocks from the Grant home. My father's voice always grew louder with each word whenever he described Carline: "But that was a school for white children, so I couldn't go to it." He then described the trek: "In the morning, we took two different streetcars and then we'd walk about one block to the school. The other possibility was the L'Ouverture School, which was almost the same distance from our home, but my parents chose Wheatley." From their seats, they would watch white children walk into half-empty classrooms.

Wheatley School, 4239 Papin Street. Photograph by Emil Boehl, ca. 1895.
Missouri History Museum.

Each afternoon, the "ticket girl" at Wheatley handed out two slips of paper—one for the trip home and another for the next morning's return—to the Grant children and anyone else in similar circumstances. "We got on the bus and paid our fare with these little tickets. There was nobody to tell us when to get on, or how to get on, or when to get off. And on one occasion, I remember, just after they introduced these trailer streetcars, Johnny got his head caught in between two of the doors and he got injured," as my father told it.

Their mother and their grandmother, Eliza Ann Collins Holliday, a former slave from Mississippi who lived with them, had total control over the children's "goings" to school but not over their "comings." After school, the Grant clan would pawn their tickets for 2 cents' worth of candy at the corner confectionery near the school and take a shortcut home by following the railroad tracks. "We had two or three near misses because there were twelve, maybe fifteen rows of main-line tracks and they were heavily trafficked in those days. We were lucky enough to get through without any of us getting seriously injured or, worse yet, killed," my father recalled.

Although none of the children got hurt on their daily constitutional home, the oldest would soon be plucked from the pack. Vivian was withdrawn from Wheatley one fall and enrolled in a "special" school for slow learners at the insistence of her teachers. They convinced my grandmother that, after two or three years of schooling there, Vivian would be able to matriculate again at Wheatley and graduate. As the boys kicked the autumn leaves alongside the railroad tracks after school one afternoon, my father blurted out, "I miss Vivian."

"Betcha don't miss getting beat up over her, do you?" Willie chided.

Eliza Ann Collins Holliday with her daughter Ruth Ann Holliday, ca. 1893.
Courtesy of Ann Camille Saunders.

Daddy grew pale at the thought of how many fights he'd lost defending his sister. He was small for his age and much younger than most of Vivian's tormentors. Even so, he always stood up for her. Once anyone called her "crazy," he would start swinging. By the time it was over, he was either "seeing double or damn near deaf," he remembered. "They'd always manage to hit me in the eye or the ear. And if you get hit real GOOD in the ear, it'll ring for a month. And as soon as they hit me in the eye, I'd see four or five of them and that was it for me."

But he still longed to walk beside her and feel like a man who could take care of her. He loved to watch her moonlike face that waxed and waned so easily. He marveled at how utterly predictable she was: The penny treats they bought each day made her beam; Willie's teasing made her cry; playing the piano made her smile; and sitting in a classroom made her stare into space. Vivian did return to Wheatley—in time to see each of her three brothers finish while she waded through scholastic waters still too deep for her. She finally managed to get her diploma—at age eighteen—with the assistance of my father, who tutored her in reading and math.

My father usually got a bit agitated when we talked about Vivian, especially when I once insisted on knowing what was "wrong" with my aunt. He raised his voice and said, "Now, I don't know what all happened but it was obvious from the beginning that she just couldn't do the work." He went on to explain, "Maybe they just gave her the degree. Hell, I don't know but I thought I was helping her at the time. I graduated two years early, was already a freshman in high school and thought I actually knew something. So I tried my hand at teaching her. They called people like Vivian mentally defective back then. But oh, how she struggled. Once she finished Wheatley, Mama kept her home from high school because she didn't want to embarrass her."

Vivian Grant at Wheatley School's graduation, 1915.

So now, the Grant boys ambled home without Vivian and rode the streetcar by themselves in the morning. "I always used to laugh about the squabble over busing in the 1960s. How neighborhoods would be *damaged* if children had to go elsewhere to school. How busing is wrong. What a joke! The authorities couldn't WAIT to bus us out of our neighborhood and gladly PAY for it! I was bused, unsupervised, mind you, from kindergarten days through my entire St. Louis primary and secondary schooling," he emphasized.

Most black and poor white adolescents faced a crucial decision when they finished elementary school. "Are you going to high school or to work?" they asked one another. Fifteen was the average age for grade school graduation, and child labor laws were still not being strictly enforced. The Grants, however, had no choice as far as their parents were concerned. They were going to high school, and the ride would become even longer. Sumner High School, the only colored secondary school in town, was more than four miles away from their home. The school board absolved itself of any responsibility for transportation costs. Parents would have to buy the tickets if they wanted their children to ride to school; otherwise their kids would have to walk, which many did. My father and his brothers rose even earlier for a longer ride on two streetcars, followed by a short walk to the school. Almost as soon as they boarded the first one, they watched white students enter the front doors of Central High School, a scant five blocks from their house.

Daddy's parents divorced when he was almost four years old. When he started grade school, he and his siblings were living with their mother, one of her brothers who was unable to work, their grandmother and, at some point, an aunt. My grandparents would remarry about six years later, only to have my grandfather,

David M. Grant at his graduation from Wheatley School, 1914. Courtesy of the Moorland-Spingarn Research Center, Howard University, Washington, D.C., Mildred H. Grant Collection.

William S. Grant, die a few years after that. Before their papa returned home, he went to Chicago intermittently and may have only sporadically sent money to his family. My father never talked about that. He made it clear that his papa passed on a skill that would afford the entire household all of the creature comforts, even though he left home without knowing about the livelihood he had left them: the practice of chiropody.

William S. Grant (David M. Grant's father), ca. 1913.

What it was and how it came about became a staple of my father's vast collection of stories and testified to my grandfather's ingenuity. Shortly after Daddy's birth, his father was employed as a bathhouse attendant at the newly opened, whites-only, Missouri Athletic Club. Cleaning up after the city's elite paid little and was appreciated even less. All that changed when my grandfather devised a service that showered him with tips. As the members finished their bathing ritual, he would wrap their feet in hot towels, shave their corns and calluses, and finish his treatment with a foot massage. He became so good at it and so praised at the club that he decided to open a private practice as a chiropodist through his knack for "fixing feet." He bolstered his reputation when he bought a gilt-framed diploma, written in Latin, from a local pawnshop and audaciously hung it in his office. His business card showcased his familiarity with an unexplained "New Scientific Method." He kept early morning, late afternoon, and Sunday office hours so he could stay on at the athletic club and collect a salary and mounting tips. Without one official day of study, my grandfather established himself as Dr. Grant, surgeon-chiropodist.

My father assured us that his dad's journey from attendant to "doctor" began at the Missouri Athletic Club, but I recently discovered otherwise. My grandparents courted for slightly less than two years before they wed in the fall of 1896, during which time they carried on a fairly extensive written correspondence. I was able to draw a fuller picture of my grandfather's rise up the economic ladder once I happened to find some of his letters. Besides pledging unshakeable devotion to his future wife, "Will" told her about his work at hotel "baths" downtown and his quest for financial stability. His notes usually began with "My Own True One" or "My Dear Sweetheart." One of his letters, dated January 26, 1896, speaks of his hoping to get a new "situation" so that he could see her more often and not be financially embarrassed. He must have been hired, because two days later his love note was written on St. James Hotel letterhead and reads: "If you have no objection I would like to take you to the Theater Thur. evening."

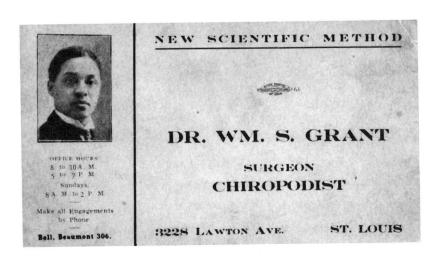

Business card of William S. Grant, chiropodist, ca. 1906. Courtesy of the Moorland-Spingarn Research Center, Howard University, Washington, D.C., Mildred H. Grant Collection.

Throughout the spring of that year, letters came, either posted with 2-cent stamps to her house, or delivered by someone's hand "At Home" or "At School" (Sumner High). All arrived on stationery etched with the hotel's logo. They attest to his determination to wed her, and to his erratic work schedule that often prevented their getting together. On May 10, 1896, he wrote, "I know you will be angry with me but dear, your Will worked very hard last night . . . that I hardly think I will be able to get out to the Park today . . . and I was feeling so very happy all day thinking that I would see you but alas it is but a dream. I will see you sweetheart after school Monday now don't worry because I have disapointed [*sic*] you today because you know doing this work, if I don't rest why I will be sick that's all." Two months earlier, he abruptly ended a four-page letter by saying, "Well I must close as it is very early in the morning and Judge Noonan is just entering the door for a bath." On May 4, he wrote, "O my dear I am over rejoiced because I passed the examination at the Post Office, things are gradually coming my way and it is only a matter of time before I can accomplish what I want to do,—and of course you know what that is my dear. In fact sometimes I wish you would come down town with me, get the license [to] marry down town and thus be united forever, why I make enough now to take care of you sweetheart indeed I do."

By late summer, he must not have become a postal clerk, which was the top of the employment rock for Negroes in those days, because his letters carried the Southern Hotel's address and logo. Its tagline, "Absolutely Fire Proof," was reassuring, given its namesake had been leveled by a blaze in 1877. In one of these, Will complained that rowdy colleagues were preventing him from seeing "Lizzie" more often. He wrote, ". . . it almost seems impossible for me to get a glimpse of you any more. Evry [*sic*] time I have an engagement I am compelled to stay on watch, I would have come out the other night but two of the boys were discharged, cause quarrelling. I had to remain on the late watch."

They finally wed in the fall of 1896 as my grandmother began her final year at Sumner, and Will's letters to Ms. Lizzie Holliday stopped; instead she received news from her girlfriends and relatives (inside and outside of St. Louis) addressed to Mrs. William Grant or Mrs. Elizabeth Grant at their home on Sixteenth

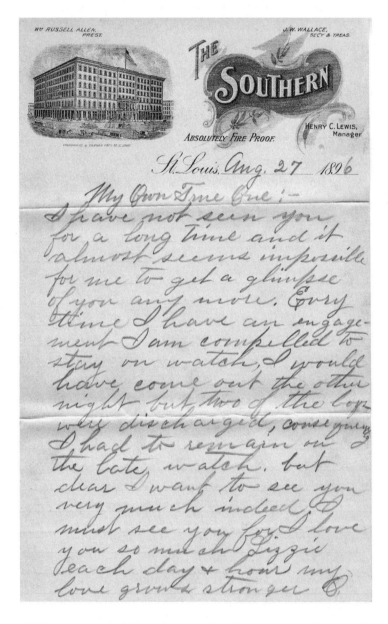

William S. Grant's letter on Southern Hotel letterhead to his future wife,
Elizabeth Holliday, August 27, 1896.

Street. The letters from my grandfather began again, however, just after the turn of the twentieth century. His drinking had become a problem, and my grandmother took her three children and moved in with her sister Mattie and her husband in Galesburg, Illinois, for a few months. Will pleaded with her to return to him, and she did, but several years later they divorced. By 1907, Lizzie was a single mother of four and the sole breadwinner for a household of seven or sometimes eight.

"Right after my father went away," Daddy recalled, "one of his clients showed up looking for him. My mother had watched Papa work and told his client that she could fix feet just as well as her husband. So that's what she did. And she became quite proficient at it." He remembered that, in a good month, she would bring home up to $500, a handsome sum by any measure in those days. Eventually, all of the boys, my father included, attended chiropody school. Johnny and Willie became chiropodists while my father went on to law school. Through William Grant's resourcefulness, a family profession was born.

Elizabeth Grant now had a skill that equipped her to care for her family and give them an upper-middle-class lifestyle: a three-story home, a well-stocked pantry, music lessons for all four children, a wardrobe full of tailored suits and high-topped shoes for the boys, silk and satin dresses with hair ribbons to match for Vivian, and bus money to get to Sumner. In the early 1920s, my grandmother was "grandfathered" into the profession when chiropodists had to be licensed. By that time, she and Will had remarried and lived again as man and wife for four years when he passed away in 1916. "He died a young man, even though forty-three seemed so old to me at the time. I got the death certificate, which said acute dilation of the heart—whatever the hell that meant," my father explained.

The Grant children, ca. 1908. Front row: David M. and John; back row: William and Vivian. Courtesy of Moorland-Spingarn Research Center, Howard University, Washington, D.C., Mildred H. Grant Collection.

My grandmother ultimately rented a small downtown office in Nugent's Department Store, where she practiced for more than twenty years until the store shut down during the Depression, but she began her professional career by making house calls. She counted the Anheuser family of beer fame among her patients, as well as others who also lived on Lindell Boulevard, the street that borders Forest Park on the north and remains famous for its nineteenth-century mansions and half-acre front lawns. She traveled by streetcar to her appointments and always dressed in black when she worked, sporting a floor-length dress, broad-brimmed hat, and in foul weather, a coat that skirted her hem. She kept her bus fare in a miniature purse fastened to a silver chain that hung around her neck and fell far below her waist, and she buried her earnings inside the pockets of her voluminous uniform. Some of the family portraits show an elegant woman dressed in pastels, but when she worked, her outfits screamed, "I am only and all about business!" In addition, her regal posture and attitude commanded respect; no one dared to call her anything other than "Madam Grant." Rumors circulated that while she had her clients "under the knife," she would tell them how much her forebears had suffered during slavery at the hands of whites. She may not have gotten much sympathy, but she certainly got paid.

Their house, just west of William Grant's first office and their previous home, was orderly and filled with music. Eliza Ann handled most of the cooking and cleaning while my grandmother rode the streetcars to her rich white clients' homes or took appointments at her downtown office for the less well heeled. The children each played a musical instrument: my father, the cello; Vivian, the piano; Johnny, the bass fiddle. William distinguished himself as a violinist who would eventually lead a jazz band. Daddy said his oldest brother was so proficient that "he could squeeze the tears out of a violin."

"We had to make our own music. We didn't have radio and TV. The phonograph was just beginning to come around so anything like that—you had to do it yourself," my father reminded me. "Before Papa left for Chicago, he and some of his friends belonged to the Bass Clef Club, a group of mostly tenors, who would gather and sing together to entertain themselves. My grade school principal, Arthur Freeman, George L. Vaughn,[1] and three or four others, I can't remember, all formed this club. I'm not sure if Gerald Tyler, who was in charge of music at Sumner, was in that group. He was quite a composer. He also directed the boys' choir at All Saints Episcopal Church. We in the boys' choir would sing one or another of his compositions on Christmas Eve at Midnight Mass."

After Midnight Mass, the Grant children would rush home. Bundled up and running on the snowy streets and alongside the horse-carried sleighs, they envisioned the hearty meal and foamy eggnog that awaited them. "It would be quite a group of eight or ten people at Mama's house. All would come by to eat and drink eggnog after the church service around 1 or 2 o'clock in the morning. She would let us have a little of it but she gave us the kind without liquor. She was dead set against alcohol because of Papa and the trouble he had with it. See, today, everybody talks about the dope scene, and back then, when I came along, there wasn't any damn dope—it was alcohol, whiskey, *demon* rum," Daddy explained.

Madam Grant insisted that her sons get an education so "you won't ever have to ask anybody for a job." She first sent William to the New England Conservatory of Music in Boston to study music. By the early 1920s, he and Johnny joined each other

---

[1] Attorney George L. Vaughn argued and won *Shelley v. Kraemer* before the U.S. Supreme Court in 1948. The landmark St. Louis case declared restrictive covenants unenforceable.

*The Grant family, ca. 1909. Left to right: William, David M.,
Madam Elizabeth, Vivian, and John.*

Chicago at the Illinois School of Chiropody, and indeed they never
applied for a job anywhere. Johnny practiced chiropody, mostly
in St. Louis, and Willie opened an office in Montreal, Canada,
where he ultimately settled. She also handed out the same advice
to each one as he left home. "She was militant and taught me to
believe that I was as good as anyone, skin color regardless."

Vivian remained at home with her mother. My grandmother
never fully accepted the "mentally defective" label affixed to her
daughter in grade school and conducted a relentless search for an

answer in one religion after the other. She abandoned All Saints Episcopal in favor of more and more fundamentalist faiths, and in due course solved the mystery. Vivian was different because she had a "special" blessing from the Lord. Gratified now, my grandmother took Vivian to an evangelistic gathering every Sunday for the rest of her life, where her daughter was treated with almost saintly reverence. My aunt was pleased to trail her mother everywhere she went, play the piano, and do whatever her little brother "Davey" requested of her in later years—from carrying a protest sign to holding forth on a picket line.

My father, on the other hand, felt prepared to work as soon as he finished high school in 1918 and persuaded his mother that college could wait.

3.

Heart to Hart
and Stem to Stern

$\mathcal{M}$Y FATHER'S FIRST JOB ENDED WITH SUCH A THUD that his remembrance of it would jar him for decades. His mother hadn't even wanted him to work so soon after graduating from high school. He was only fifteen years old and still looked like a preteen, so she wanted him at home with her for a while before he did anything or went anywhere.

But it was 1918 and World War I was raging. My father put it this way: "Boys had to mature into men and take on the responsibilities of grown men because they had all gone to the war. And the railroad industry was desperate for able-bodied men to wait tables, change linens, cook food—make the trains run."

So he convinced his mother to let him apply for a position as a club car porter on the Wabash Railroad and got the job on the spot. In those days, according to my father, club car porters were a particular breed. They only worked on the midnight-to-dawn part of the run, like the night trains between St. Louis and Kansas City, and St. Louis and Chicago. Each trip took about six or seven hours. Some passengers would sit up for the ride in coach seats, and others would recline in a Pullman car with its pull-down, bunklike beds or individual sleeping compartments. A club car porter was assigned to the rear half of a coach car, which took up about fifteen to twenty feet of the car. It was there for the convenience of the Pullman passengers in the car behind it. In fact, the coach passengers were not even supposed to enter it.

"It was my job to serve them food. I worked in a kitchen about the size of a broom closet, but you'd be surprised at what they could put inside. They were absolute magicians at storing things. I'd have canned tongue, ham, eggs, bacon, a few tins of beans. I could make sandwiches and so on. Not a lot, but one man could do the whole thing. There were no alcoholic drinks because Prohibition was in the offing, and besides, a minor couldn't serve drinks."

My father also had to master an inventory sheet that measured between four and five feet wide and up to three feet long. It was the same form used on full-blown dining cars. Once a month, porters had to account for each and every item that came in or left their hold. My father became so skilled at preparing it that, on occasion, his duties included training the older dining car stewards on how to fill it out. This "damned thing," as Daddy called it, eventually would be his undoing.

My father didn't think much about the work, just did his job and was glad to be making his own money. But even as a teenager, he noticed how unfairly the Negro employees were treated. "Well, back in those days, they had no unions of any kind. And it was pretty terrible. Men, grown men with families at home, wives and children, could be let go at any time for no reason. Just on the whim of the commissary chief."

During Daddy's employment, the commissary chief was a man named Hart. "He was a veritable Simon Legree. A big, evil-looking white man with a large mole on the left side of his face. I never will forget the bastard. Cooks, waiters were all scared to death of him; he was a demon."

Hart's reputation preceded him, and each new employee heard, more or less, the same story. Tall and beefy, he would show up on a train, unannounced, looking to fire someone. He'd pick out some colored cook or waiter or porter and yell at him. According to my father, an exchange like this followed:

"You, there! How long you been on here?"

"Fourteen years, sir," came a possible reply.

"Well, you've been on this car too long. You probably think you OWN this car," Hart usually ranted.

Before long, Hart would sack the man for no reason. "So when anybody got a letter in his box telling him to report to the commissary office, those poor fellas would almost go into nervous fits. As far as I was concerned, this job didn't mean a damned thing to me; it was just a lark. Mama would have preferred that I didn't work anyhow," Daddy recounted.

Hart had a white boy working for him named Francis English. He was seventeen or eighteen years old and still in high school. Periodically, he would come to check my father's list against the receipts since a porter also served as cashier. They worked well together. Since Daddy had already graduated, he had no special regard for English and actually felt superior to him. At one point, something happened to a can of beans. My father recorded it and reported the accident to English. After the next run, one of Hart's dreaded letters showed up in Daddy's mailbox.

Hart's office was inside a wood-frame building, far south of the railroad station. "It was a grimy, greasy little old building with a long, dark hall that led to Hart's office," as my father described it.

As Daddy approached the commissary, he knew that Hart would take him for a thief, but since he had explained everything to his pal, Francis, he was confident that the episode would be easily settled. He had nothing to fear, he told himself, as he entered Hart's office and the chief inquired about the beans. "Well, Mr. Hart, I told Francis about that when he came to check my inventory," he explained. Hart immediately snapped at him:

"What did you call him?"

"Francis," Daddy answered.

"Well, you call him Mr. English, you hear," Hart responded.

"Mr. Hart, I call him Francis on the car, and he doesn't complain."

At this point, Hart stood up from his chair and shouted: "Don't you tell me about that. Remember, you are a common nigger club car porter and he is my secretary and a white man. You call him Mr. English and don't you EVER forget it." My father usually roared out these lines.

But then my dad's normally robust voice habitually weakened ever so slightly as he explained the next chapter: "Well, I got the keys out of my pocket because a lump came in my throat that I knew I couldn't swallow and I was so hurt. I knew I was going to cry. And I didn't want him to see me cry. I put the keys on his desk and I said, 'Mr. Hart, I quit.'" He turned on his heel and walked down the hallway.

Once out of Hart's earshot, he stopped. "I stood in that hall and I cried like a baby. I, I, I've never been so hurt like that in my life," he told me. As soon as he stopped sobbing, he descended the rickety steps and went straight to his mother's office to tell her what happened. As Madam Grant stared into the bloodshot eyes of her baby, she held back enough tears to flood the banks of the Mississippi River. A white man had just insulted her baby, and there was nothing she could say or do about it. Her only weapon was leashed fury.

But my father's story didn't stop there, and his tone regained its usual dynamism. The sequel happened more than twenty years later, and his amusement in telling it was infectious. By then, Daddy was an assistant city counselor for the City of St. Louis. He and his brother Johnny were dining at Fred Harvey's restaurant in the Union Station, which was the only white-owned dining room in town where Negroes could be served. When they finished and left the restaurant, my father eyed a man down the mall. "C'mon, Johnny. Let's go 'cause I got an old score to settle," he said excitedly.

They rushed toward the man, and he turned out to be Hart.

"My name's Grant. You probably wouldn't remember me, but I could NEVER forget you. Didn't you have a white fella working for you named Francis English? I mean, MISTER Francis English?"

"Yes, I remember him," Hart agreed.

Daddy gave him a blow-by-blow account of the incident. "After you called me a common nigger club car porter, I went back to school because I didn't want to go through life with white men like you calling me names like that. And if you hadn't said that to me, I guess I'd still be riding up and down on that damned car of yours. And now, Mr. Hart, I'm a lawyer for the City of St. Louis. I probably make a bigger salary than you do. And I owe every bit of it to you, sir. And I'd made my mind up that the first time I saw you, I'd THANK you for what you did for me." By the time Daddy finished thrashing him verbally, Hart was speechless.

He once again turned on his heel and walked away. Instead of tears flowing from his eyes, sparks were flying. He enjoyed nothing more than winning a battle with words and cunning. He knew his mother, who was largely responsible for his schooling, wouldn't mind how he had just skewered the truth. His more cautious brother was shocked.

"My God, Dave, you will give that man a stroke," Johnny worried. "That was so bitter."

"Well, I don't give a damn if he does and I'll tell you one thing. I bet that'll stop him from calling Negroes names like that because he'll be afraid that he'll run them back to school." They both exploded in laughter as they strolled out of the station that night.

This tale still didn't end. The *Negro Digest,* which black publishing legend John Johnson founded before *Ebony* and *Jet* magazines, had a column titled "My Most Humiliating Jim Crow Experience." It invited comments from Negroes to describe a racial insult. Daddy wrote up the incident but suggested that the magazine retitle its column. "My Best Remembered Victory over Jim Crow" seemed more fitting to him. They didn't change the name but carried his story and sent him a check for $10. "And that's the way she goes," he said as he finished this tale. He concluded so many of his stories with this unexplained punctuation mark, even though I could often figure out what it meant. Sometimes it was filled with irony, other times in resignation, or in this instance, a straightforward "gotcha!"

My father's days of staying at home and recovering from Mr. Hart's nastiness were short lived. He longed to "see the world" and soon persuaded his mother to let him join a crew headed to Detroit for work on a steamboat called the *Tashmoo.* The White Star Line, its owner, had put out a call for waiters, and he hoped that his club car porter experience would help him master a weightier kind of service. The boat carried passengers back and forth between Detroit, Michigan, and Sarnia, Ontario, on a daily basis. After several mishaps, he managed to become a full-fledged waiter. His days on the *Tashmoo* were also numbered; he worked there for only sixteen of them, just long enough to pay back the company the railroad fare it had advanced him to get to Detroit. "I remember exactly what that was—$16.01 from St. Louis to Detroit in coach," he said.

The steamer Tashmoo, *the first Great Lake boat David M. Grant worked on, from a 1914 postcard.*

He quit because he learned quickly that boats crisscrossed the Great Lakes all summer long and they all needed somebody to carry a tray. His adventuresome spirit took over and he transferred to another line and the chance to go from Detroit to Buffalo, New York. His last run on that boat turned into grist for another story. After riding for a while on that run, a new headwaiter came on board. "I think I dropped a platter on someone's head. I don't quite remember what happened but I sure as hell know that in the middle of Lake Erie, he decided to demote me and told me I'd bus dishes from then on," Daddy recounted.

My father considered himself to be first-rate at his job in spite of the disobedient platter and refused; in fact, he quit his job and went to his bunk! As the ship pulled into the Buffalo harbor the next morning, a policeman awaited him. He boarded the vessel, escorted David Grant, delinquent busboy, off the boat, and charged him with mutiny on the high seas. "They clearly wanted to make an example out of me. 'What if the captain quit or the chief pilot?' they told me. At any rate, it threw a scare into me and when we got back to Detroit, I did quit that boat although I had already 'been quit,' if you know what I mean," he chuckled.

He spent the balance of the summer zigzagging across the Great Lakes, running from one lakeside city to the next. As September approached and the summer boat season concluded, he learned that the colored waiters would head south to the Arlington Hotel in Hot Springs, Arkansas, and as spring blossomed, they would take off for French Lick, Indiana. After that, they would return to Detroit and start their "year" all over again. "So, it looked like that was going to be my life's work. I did go to Hot Springs and to French Lick, and then I returned to Detroit. In between times, I would go home to see my family. And my mother would give me hell about going back to school. She was a great one for education, but I was foolish and wasn't thinking about anything like that," he told me.

His boating days would come to an abrupt halt after two years of wandering from one port of call to another, trying to quench his wanderlust. He signed on to the Northern Navigation Line, a Canadian outfit that held sway over many of the northern ports of the lakes. One of the deputy mates was incensed that Negro boys waited tables, feeling these jobs rightfully belonged to Canadian whites. He took his bigoted attitude out on any colored male in the dining room. Before long, my father and the Canadian came to blows. Daddy's size always put him at a disadvantage, yet this fight was one of the few physical battles he ever won in his life. But it almost cost him an eye.

"I'd thrown him down, and we were wrestling on the ground. Somehow he managed to get hold of my eye. I guess he was trying to pull it out. But anyway, he squeezed the side of my eye enough to damage it, not the eyeball itself but the side. I threw one last punch that stunned him and headed for the flicker, which is what they called where we stayed. I looked at this thing in the mirror and I got awfully furious," Daddy explained.

Once he returned to Detroit, he decided to buy a gun and go looking for his rival. He'd won the fight but would surely lose his job, and "nobody would run me off a boat," he affirmed. But then he took a detour that possibly saved his life or at least kept him out of jail. He opted to stop by the rooming house where he kept a room so as not to be known as a "boat rat." Anyone who didn't have a bed on dry land received that nickname. It only cost $6 or $7 per week. His landlady's eyes bugged once she saw his face but rather than gasp aloud, she quickly said, "I've got a surprise for you!"

"And I bet I know what it is. Is my mother here?" Madam Grant, as most mothers, had the uncanny ability to intervene whenever he needed her. She looked at him squarely and said, "What happened?" My father inhaled deeply and came up with a whopper of a lie. If she knew he'd been in a fight, he knew she wouldn't let him out of her sight until he was twenty-one. He spun a yarn full of minute details about how the lake had gotten rough and how the waiters scrambled to clear the tables of silver-ware and water bottles to keep the dining room as tidy as possible during the "storm." All of a sudden, a wave hit the boat and my father went flying, clipping the corner of his eye against the side of a table. She listened and said, "Well, you are through with these boats because you are going back to school."

He and his mother boarded a train the next day for Ann Arbor, Michigan, where she enrolled him in the University of Michigan's School of Liberal Arts as a freshman. It was 1920. "If she hadn't come up to Detroit and slammed me into Michigan, I could have spent what was left of my life hating myself, maybe as a headwaiter in some dining room, serving other people food," he concluded. "God praise her for having done that."

Out of a student population of twelve thousand to fourteen thousand, there were about fifty to sixty Negroes at Michigan. Belford V. Lawson, who became a famous civil rights attorney in Washington, D.C., was among them. He was the first Negro varsity football player at Michigan. Daddy would talk about how he and his friends tried to cheer on Belford by coming to football practice and scrimmages. "They'd beat the hell out of him, and he would keep coming back for more. Belford never complained; that's how much he wanted to play for Michigan," Daddy always said.

Most of the Negro students worked their way through college as busboys, dishwashers, and waiters. My father did the latter but, even so, more work on a boat awaited him; this time, however, he would be treated like a passenger and served his meals at a linen-laden table. His oldest brother, Willie, fresh from studying violin in Boston, preferred jazz to the classics. By the time Daddy finished freshman year, his brother had put together a band that serenaded passengers on the *Majestic* steamer. Its route took passengers up and down the Mississippi River from New Orleans to Dubuque, Iowa. Willie easily persuaded my father, with his meager skills on the cello, to come along. He and the band members became the prima donnas of the boat because, as Daddy put it, "Your paddle can be as fit as any, but if you haven't got a good

David M. Grant and his mother, Elizabeth Holliday Grant, ca. 1918.
Courtesy of the Moorland-Spingarn Research Center, Howard University,
Washington, D.C., Mildred H. Grant Collection.

band on a night excursion cruise, you just don't have a boat that's worth anything." So they'd play until late in the evening, never eat breakfast, and rarely see daylight before eleven o'clock. By that time, lunch awaited them. They'd rehearse for a few hours and then lounge around the boat watching the white cabin boys do all of the cleaning. "And I'd never been looked at more angrily than by them. Remember, the boat left port in Louisiana," he explained.

When they landed in Natchez, their stroll into town became circuslike. "We were dressed in suits and ties, and it seemed like every white person who saw us stopped and gawked. People even came out of their homes and stores to stare and point and whisper to each other. I guess it was because all of the colored men were in overalls," he recounted. "The white people looked at us like they'd seen a mirage."

After three years at Michigan, my father quit school. "Mama had Johnny and Willie both in chiropody school in Chicago and, frankly, I thought the load was a little heavy." She would have gladly carried the financial burden and was disappointed to see her youngest child take jobs unworthy of him. He went back to the railroad and the lake boats, and he also worked as a drill press and crane operator in Detroit. While riding the rails, this time as a waiter and club and private car porter on the Missouri Pacific and the Santa Fe lines, he saw that working conditions for Negro employees were still appalling. Any white man—a Pullman car conductor, brakeman, or train conductor—could have any colored man fired on impulse. Pullman car porters, who held the most prestigious jobs, received an average of $810 per year. In order to get paid at all, they had to work four hundred hours a month (sometimes as much as twenty nonstop) or cover eleven thousand miles on board, whichever came first. When George

Pullman revolutionized train travel with his invention of sleeping cars in 1867, his company would lease Pullman cars to a railroad, fully equipped with staff. He used recently freed slaves, judging them to be skilled in service and willing to work for next to nothing. Pullman decided that they should be called by his first name. All of these "Georges" topped off their pay through tips and tried to outdo each other by offering top-notch service and by competing for runs known for carrying big-spending travelers. They were not paid for any work carried out before noon, even if their train left the station at eight in the morning. Oftentimes, the company demanded that they arrive long before the run started or their hours began to be counted, in order to outfit the cars with fresh linens, towels, and so on. They had to pay for their uniforms, shoe polish, and meals and were allowed short naps in the smoking car.

As a waiter, Daddy took his meals in the kitchen, usually standing. It would be years before the waitstaff could sit down in the dining car after finishing their work. Even then, they were instructed to pull the shades when passing through the South; otherwise whites along the road would throw bricks at the windows.

Even though Pullman car porters were admired in their home communities because they had a stable wage, had an opportunity to travel throughout the country, and enjoyed work largely free of manual labor (rare for colored men in those days), they suffered continual indignities. No better than poorly paid bellhops in what George Pullman called "a hotel on wheels," the workers decided to take on the company by forming a union in 1925, the Brotherhood of Sleeping Car Porters. Pullman immediately commenced wholesale firings of anyone who joined. My father's distrust of corporations and admiration for unions grew during those years and eventually he would call himself a "union man."

As he rode the rails and watched a revolution in the making, he had no idea how much he would contribute to its outcome.

"I took a year of chiropody up there in Chicago where my brothers studied but didn't finish the course. By 1927, I'd been out of high school for nine years and I realized that the train was about to leave me at the station if I didn't get on board and do something more with my life." So he resolved to take on a profession or else he would be doomed to filling out job applications.

Without much thought, he chose law because, as he always said, "I remembered those medical students at Michigan. How they'd come back to the dorm with boxes of bones. They had to learn where all of the muscles and ligaments went in and out of them. I knew I wasn't up for that." In those days, an undergraduate degree was not required to study law; one only needed enough college credits to qualify, which my father had. So he applied and was accepted at Howard University in Washington, D.C. "Separate but equal" education for Negroes was still legal and mandated in some states, including Missouri. If a Negro wanted to study a course offered at the University of Missouri but not at Lincoln University, the colored college in Jefferson City, the state would pay his or her tuition to attend an out-of-state institution. The policy didn't affect my father when he attended Michigan because his liberal arts curriculum could be had at Lincoln; but Lincoln had no faculty of jurisprudence, so Missouri paid my father to go to Howard. "It was a very unsatisfactory thing; they never appropriated enough money and each time I went, I had to pay my tuition and then later I'd get it back at Howard," he explained.

When Daddy left for Howard, in a funny sort of way, he got "bused" all over again to go to school.

4.

UPSTAIRS/DOWNSTAIRS

Recollections of an Embalmer's Daughter

Y MOTHER'S UPBRINGING WAS, IN SOME WAYS, DRA-
matically different from my father's. She never
rode public transportation or walked anywhere without holding
her father's hand or being accompanied by one of her parents'
employees. She usually began her stories in the same way.

"All I remember is being driven there in a limousine by
Nathaniel, the chauffeur." This was her surprisingly brief recollection of her first years at Waring Elementary School in St. Louis
during the 1920s. In spite of my mother's colossal memory of
just about everything else, she came up short when talking about
primary school. Perhaps she recalled so little because, as she put
it, "there was so much going on at home."

My mother grew up at 2620 Lawton Avenue in a row house
not unlike many on the east side of Grand Avenue and, coinci-
dentally, only a few blocks from where her future husband was
born. It was a solid neighborhood of working-class people, some
of whom, with new paychecks in hand, "acted up" a bit on Saturday night. Otherwise, they went about their business within
the broad mix of trades and professions that characterized pre-

integration black neighborhoods. She was reared in relative luxury as the babied only child of the proprietors of a funeral parlor. Her parents, Lyda (née Franklin) and John Hughes, had owned a bar until my grandmother broke through a social barrier and became one of the first Negro female embalmers in the state of Missouri. While the J. W. Hughes Funeral Home carried her husband's name, she oversaw nearly every aspect of its operation. She received her license in the early 1920s after studying at the Eckles School of Embalming in Pennsylvania; shortly thereafter, my grandmother's leap of faith turned into a well-regarded undertaking establishment.

My grandparents' staff included four full-time employees: Oni, the cook and housekeeper; Nathaniel, the chauffeur; Douglas, the janitor; and Big Will, a woman whom Lyda had brought from Oklahoma as my mother's nursemaid at the behest of Big Will's son, Cass, who worked part-time at the home. They all shamelessly doted on my mother while Boots, her shiny black cocker spaniel, trailed her dutifully, except when she had him flattened to the ground when she tried to "ride" him around the neighborhood. Grandma's girlfriends were equally enamored of Mother. They belonged to the Daughters of the Improved Benevolent Protective Order of Elks of the World (Black Elks), the sister organization to a black men's fraternity, and they adopted little Mildred as their mascot.

The funeral parlor and business offices occupied the ground floor of the three-story, brick building. My grandparents and mother lived on the second floor, and Oni and Big Will resided above them. The morgue was situated in the basement, where Douglas stayed, and Nathaniel lived on his own. Back then, both wakes and church services often occurred in one place—the funeral home—since most of the small, albeit numerous, store-

Lyda Franklin Hughes with her daughter, Mildred, dressed for a Black Elks parade. Photograph by Maxwell's, 1920s. Courtesy of the Moorland-Spingarn Research Center, Howard University, Washington, D.C., Mildred H. Grant Collection.

front churches that dotted Negro St. Louis's landscape in the 1920s were too cramped to accommodate all of the mourners. A typical church in those days was similar to the one that Philip Lee Scott founded in his living room at 2621 Lawton Avenue, just across the street from my mother's home. He advertised his Lively Stone Church of God, now a Baptist mainstay in St. Louis, by posting a small sign in front of his residence.

In any event, the vigils usually took place between seven and nine o'clock the night before the religious service. The various Baptist, Methodist, and African Methodist Episcopal (AME) preachers would officiate the next morning. If the deceased did not belong to a church, my grandfather would conduct a service, say a few words, and read from the family Bible that stood atop the funeral parlor lectern. He always extended condolences and a steady arm for the bereaved to cling to. The women mourners brought enough food and soft drinks to serve everyone. Although Grandma categorically banned bootleg liquor from the home itself, the men would sip it surreptitiously on the steps outside, and the spirits obviously added a certain élan to their grieving. My mother looked forward to each wake because she loved peeping stealthily over the banister from her perch on the second-floor landing. "For a child, it was exciting to listen to the spirituals and watch the people get happy and jump up and carry on."

Sometimes, however, she did not get to enjoy her bird's-eye view because certain wakes took place away from the funeral parlor. Ordinarily, Nathaniel would drive the dead wagon (a wagon-like vehicle that was used to pick up corpses and take them to the funeral parlor to be embalmed) to the coroner's, the hospital, or the home of the deceased to collect the remains. Occasionally in the latter event, the family members were so grief stricken that they refused to let go. So Grandma would have Nathaniel load up the dead wagon with all of her instruments, travel to the residence, and embalm the body there. Everyone in the neighborhood knew when that happened because a red danger sign and a wreath, embroidered with black ribbons, were conspicuously hung on the front door to indicate the presence of a corpse. The wake followed soon thereafter in the house. By the early 1930s, this practice ended when the City Health Department outlawed embalming at home.

When Grandma did her work at the funeral home, my mother sat with her. "At eight or nine years old, I remember playing in the morgue. It didn't bother me at all. I just liked spending time with my mother. She had this long, white, enameled table. You know, like the ones you see in an operating room. And she would show me how she did the embalming. For me, it was amazing to see everything that's inside of us."

In those days, unless a doctor was present to certify the death, the Coroner's Office took immediate possession of the body to determine the cause. In so doing, the coroner had to cut it from the clavicle to the pubic bone. He then called the family's designated funeral director. When the cadaver arrived and was laid on the table, my grandmother began her job. First, she would insert a trocar—a needle about two feet long with a circumference as large as an adult's little finger—into the open cavity. She used it to extract bodily fluids; the instrument would then be flushed out and sterilized. "And then she had, they were like IV bottles hanging there, and the embalming fluid would come down through this trocar, and she'd punch it down in the navel. Good Lord, now that I think about it—WHEW!" my mother gasped. After the liquid filled the corpse, my grandmother removed the needle, sutured the coroner's incision if need be, and hosed and dried off the body.

Then came the less taxing part of her work; she styled the hair, applied appropriate makeup, and dressed the deceased. The family had to purchase a shroud for a female. It opened down the back; was usually pink, lavender, or blue; had long sleeves with a high neck; and was pleated in front. The menswear posed a special problem because the jacket and shirt had to be cut in two down the back, so my grandmother could handily put them on. Her reputation as an expert embalmer and one who could make the dearly departed look "just like they were sleeping" spread rapidly. According to my mother, "When she got through with the people, and put makeup on, everybody always used to talk about Mrs. Hughes and what a great embalmer she was. Of course, she couldn't lift the bodies. There was a Mr. Young, who was also an embalmer, and he would assist her. But she was in charge," Mother recalled.

As soon as Grandma stopped chatting with Mommy and became engrossed in her work, my mother would often rummage around the underground office. "Sometimes I would jump on the church truck and roll around the basement while Mama worked." Composed of a metal plate, long enough to carry a coffin, atop a collapsible, accordion-like roller, the church truck was one of her favorite toys. She would also use it as part of a game she played with her mother. At some point, she would get down and, without making a sound, place the truck in one of the darkened corners. Bothered by the silence, Grandma would go searching for her daughter. As she approached, Mother would push it out of nowhere, laughing all the way. Lyda indulged her daughter each time by letting out a startled yelp. It was Mommy's way of telling her that it was time for both of them to go upstairs so she could have a snack and her mother could have her tea and take a break.

"As I look back on it, it didn't scare me at all to watch Mama do her work. Death didn't bother me until I got older. I thought the

STATEMENT

J. W. HUGHES

UNDERTAKER AND EMBALMER

LADY IN ATTENDANT: MRS. J. W. HUGHES

2620 LAWTON AVE.

ST. LOUIS. MO. ___May 11,_____ 19_55_

Mr. David M. Grant

3309 Arsenal Street

Casket	$ 735	00
Vault	150	00
Embalming	30	00
Opening grave)) Bill attached	65	00
Cleaning arrears)	73	20
Hearse @$15.00 (Donated)	15	00
Flower car @$15.00 (Donated)	15	00
Family cars 2 @$12.00 (Donated)	24	00
Burial Dress @$24.00 (Donated)	24	00
$78 00		
Family Floral	50	00
Cash advanced 5/7	200	00
Total	$1381	20
Less donations	78	00
Net balance due	$1303	20

Mrs J. W. Hughes

J. W. Hughes Funeral Home receipt for Elizabeth Holliday Grant's funeral, dated May 11, 1955.

Mildred Hughes Grant reading, ca. 1920.

whole process was really interesting, especially when they had autopsies and the person would be open from the neck all the way down. And that's when she first showed me these black lungs. I remember her saying, 'Now, you see this is what happens when you live in St. Louis.' She didn't say anything about smoking. People didn't complain about smoking back then. But they always talked about the coal."

In those days, St. Louis was covered with grime. Staunton, Illinois, had immense coal mines that furnished the surrounding communities with most of their heating needs. Its availability and low cost made bituminous, or "soft" coal, as it was known, the favored energy source of its day. With the barest breath of wind, its gritty soot traveled effortlessly and saturated the city, especially the neighborhoods bordering the river. Old-timers remember how quickly the collars and cuffs of their starched, white shirts darkened as they scurried to church in the winter as children. In addition, trains delivered coal to St. Louis, and any home close to the tracks received the lion's share of its debris. The house at 2620 Lawton lay close to this route and within walking distance from a depot where St. Louisans bought their coal. "I remember people with scuttle buckets going to get coal to heat their rooms," my mother explained. Youngsters whose parents couldn't afford coal invented a way to get some for free. They would hide under an overpass and wait for a train. Just as the engine approached, they would begin pelting bricks at the conductor and brakemen, who would return fire with chunks of coal.

Coal was brought to the funeral home each morning and dumped down a shoot in the back of the house to the basement furnace. "You can imagine the dust that came along with it," she added. Battling the soot at the funeral parlor became a daily chore. Every morning, Oni would clean off the infinite grains and tiny bits that flew through the air and had collected overnight on the deep stone window ledges and front porch stoop. Every evening, Big Will would bathe my mother, paying special attention to her belly button and the cracks between her toes where the soot would settle. During the intervening hours, Oni and Big Will and, at times, Lyda, would sweep and mop and sweep some more.

Eventually in the late 1930s, two men, one colored and one white, broke the stranglehold that soft coal had on the city and its residents. Herbert Duckett and Raymond R. Tucker, both chemical engineers for the city, devised a strategy that helped St. Louis shift to anthracite, a far less polluting sort of coal, and other forms of energy to meet its heating needs. When lit, anthracite gave off only a hint of smoke. Early environmentalists, they rode around south St. Louis on the back of a truck, explaining the hazards of soft coal. They began their campaign when the weather turned warm, assuring them of an audience since most people sat outside of their homes in an effort to beat the heat. Until their grassroots crusade, St. Louis was one of the dirtiest cities in the country. Duckett and Tucker provided the city with an invaluable service, but the issue would be catastrophic for the Democrats and become the bête noire of the 1941 election.

During the 1920s, poverty-striken Negroes wandered the streets and counted on the colored community's preachers and undertakers to offer some relief from their troubles, if only momentarily. A constant stream of these people stopped at the front door of 2620 Lawton, and Grandma gave each one a sandwich, a cool drink in the summer or a hot one in the winter, and a coin before leaving. If there was no meat or cheese on hand, she or Oni would fix a scrambled egg sandwich on the spot. One of the passersby, a man named Douglas, received more than a handout. He made such a favorable impression that the Hugheses hired him as the janitor. He remained at the "home" until he died.

My grandparents' enterprise at 2620 Lawton, however, was more than just a business; Oni, Big Will, Douglas, and Nathaniel formed part of the Hugheses' extended family. Their jobs were never in jeopardy because of whatever shortcomings they may have had. If they quit, it was their choice.

Douglas was a short, gentle man with features so keen that he resembled an Englishman wrapped in ebony. The Hugheses knew very little about his past but they soon discovered that he was an alcoholic. Whenever he went on a binge, he would either go to his room in the basement or disappear for a few days until the police picked him up and notified my grandmother. Nathaniel would then drive to get him from the drunk tank. When Douglas couldn't work, Big Will's son, Cass, or another part-timer would fill in for him. Everyone tolerated Douglas's weakness for liquor and worked around him until he sobered up and resumed his duties. He never talked about himself or invited questions about his family or background.

On the other hand, Nathaniel was talkative and loved to laugh. He maintained the home's assortment of vehicles—the Cadillac limousine that carried the deceased's family, the Nash town car that led the funeral procession, the hearse, and the ominous dead wagon. Although he worked primarily for my grandparents, they shared him with other small mortuaries and borrowed their drivers when they needed extras. Unlike the other employees, Nathaniel lived on his own. My grandparents eventually stopped buying Cadillacs altogether when money got tight; instead, they leased limos from a service run by a Negro family who bought a few cars for the exclusive use of undertakers in the area. My grandparents also disposed of the dead wagon since it was symbolic of death, and instead used the hearse, which was normally only used in funeral processions, to transport the remains.

Grandma referred to Big Will Whitfield as her daughter's nursemaid. "She takes care of Mildred," she would explain to anyone who wanted to know what she did. Her straight, down-to-the-middle-of-her-back hair; ruddy complexion; and thin lips advertised her Native American heritage and belied her African roots. Cass had pined so much for his mother, who lived in Okmulgee, Oklahoma, that my grandmother sent for her. My mother's voice always softened when she reminisced about Big Will. "I adored her. She had a very soothing presence. I loved to go up on the third floor to her room and just sit with her. We didn't talk a lot, and she didn't read to me. Maybe she couldn't read, I don't know. I liked to comb her long, thick hair and by the time I finished, it was full of knots. She always let me do it but she drew the line when I wanted to cut it. Otherwise, she was very patient with me. She stayed with us until she died." Big Will liked to swear and each time she did, my mother would fall on her knees, fold her hands, and pray to the Lord to forgive her. "Of course, she would curse on purpose just to see me do it," Mother said.

An outstanding cook, Oni "turned everything to ambrosia," my mother remembered in an almost trancelike state. Each breakfast and dinner resembled a feast. Depending on the day of the week and the season of the year, the morning meal consisted of any combination of bacon, fried ham, eggs, fried apples, French toast, pancakes, grits, pork sausage, turkey hash, fried corn, fruit juice, and coffee. A plate piled with homemade biscuits normally adorned the table until Oni rebelled and substituted toast. Grandpa insisted on salt mackerel every Sunday morning, and his wife obligingly went to the richly stocked Union Market in downtown St. Louis the day before to buy it. She soaked the fish overnight so it would be fit to eat by the next day. Dinner, always a full-blown production, became an even bigger event on Sundays when Oni trotted out fried chicken, or catfish, or baked ham, or a pot roast, or short ribs of beef, or chicken and dumplings, or smothered cabbage with ham hocks. Side dishes were drawn from string beans; turnip or mustard greens; mashed potatoes; candied sweet potatoes; pickled beets; cornbread; rolls; potato salad; macaroni and cheese; and spaghetti with onions, green peppers, and tomato sauce. When in season, lima beans, freshly popped from their shells, enhanced the menu. Oni transformed canned pineapple rings into delicacies by drenching them in batter and flash-frying them in sizzling oil. Dessert could be strawberry shortcake, a peach or blueberry cobbler, or a fried pie. Oni fashioned the latter dish, a thoroughly Southern concoction, from fresh pie dough filled with dried apricots, peaches, or apples that had been soaked, softened, and mashed with sugar, nutmeg, cinnamon, and butter. "She'd pinch the sides together and make pinpricks in it with a fork." She then dunked the bulging bag of dough in hot lard and hung it to drip before serving it. "Indescribably delicious," my mother sighed.

Oni and Big Will ate first with my grandparents and mother. The second seating included Nathaniel and Douglas and any of the part-timers who were working that day, not because of any snobbery but out of practicality: The dining table, placed in the kitchen, only sat six. Douglas, who shunned chitchat, always filled his plate and took it elsewhere to eat by himself.

Grandma made sure that Oni had the best ingredients. In early summer, she had Nathaniel drive her to a friend's farm in Michigan, a road trip that took from sunup to sundown. They returned laden with bushels of white corn, bing cherries, string beans, okra, and summer squash for the season. Five of my grandmother's eleven sisters lived in Chicago, and she stopped with one or the other of them along the way. Grandma was part of a clan of sixteen siblings born in Christiana, Tennessee, outside of Nashville. Her parents, Tennessee Kelly and Nathan Franklin, ran a

Lyda Hughes's parents from Christiana, Tennessee, Nathan Franklin and Tennessee Kelly Franklin, ca. 1900.

small farm and gravestone-carving business. Many of the children left for Chicago as soon as possible after finishing grade school, which, as in St. Louis, occurred around the age of fifteen. The first-born, Sophie, was also the first to head north. Thereafter, one by one, some of her sisters joined her, met Chicago men (also transplants from the South), and got married. My grandparents had lived for a short time in the Windy City but quickly chose St. Louis as a less hectic place to raise their daughter.

As soon as Grandma returned from Michigan with her supply of fresh produce, everything had to be cleaned, cooked, and canned immediately for winter eating. "I don't know how they did it all in that little kitchen with that tiny sink," my mother marveled. During the colder months, Grandma patronized the

Union Market, roaming from the bakery stall to the fruit racks to the vegetable bins and finally to the butcher's refrigerated glass containers.

Oni's culinary magic filled the household with the sweetest smells each morning and enticed everyone to get out of bed, even during the harshest winters. One morning, however, stood out from all of the others. As my mother lifted her nose from under the covers, expecting to be lured from her slumber, no aroma or kitchen clatter awaited her. Oni had vanished. Maybe she got tired of making all of those biscuits from scratch and frying pies. Grandma and Big Will took over and although formidable cooks themselves, the flakiness of their piecrusts never quite measured up to Oni's and the crackle of their fried chicken didn't ring out as loudly. Oni, the pretty, brown-skinned woman, departed without saying a word or leaving a forwarding address.

My grandmother had a few specialties of her own, unknown to Oni, although she wasn't always successful with them. She made root beer in the basement where it was cool and dark. If she botched a batch, she knew it by the sound of exploding bottles under her feet or because it came out flat as she poured it. The foam had to sit up high and frothy. A residue that looked like mold fell to the bottom of the glass bottles, a by-product of the fermentation process, so pouring the root beer without mixing in the sediment became an art. Furthermore, she served visitors her own brand of wine throughout the twenties. She never drank it herself, except when she made one of her weighty pound cakes. "Sometimes the cakes would fall but they were good even then," my mother laughed out. Grandma always picked grapes from the vineyard in Michigan for the wine. "She had big granite jugs where she'd let the grapes ferment." Grandma usually had a cut-glass bowl full of handpicked pecans for her guests and the household. There was a nut factory in the next block where some of the women in the neighborhood cracked, shelled, and packaged pecans day in and day out for pennies. "I guess they would slip some of the extra nuts out of the batch and bring them to Mama in a big jar because they knew how much 'Mrs. Hughes' liked them," Mother said.

Whenever I questioned my mother about prejudice in St. Louis while she was growing up, she usually discounted it. "You see, we didn't have much contact with white people." She added that other than the dealings her parents had with vendors for their business, most of whom were white, they lived comfortably within their own community. "There was one man named Harry Frank who sold automobile tires. He was Jewish, and he and Mama became good friends. They had cars, you know, and she'd buy her tires from him. They didn't have a lot of money in those days so they would put so much down and he'd come by every week or whatever and Mama would pay him."

White insurance collectors blanketed the neighborhood on a weekly basis, mainly so Negroes could keep up with their funeral premiums. "The men would go from house to house and then you'd pay for your premiums; that's how you did it. No paying through the mail," Mother said. The New York Metropolitan Life Insurance Company sent out a legion of foot soldiers to collect, anywhere from 5 to 25 cents a week, so colored people would be assured of a proper burial. "Mama and Daddy could have gotten into funeral insurance but that would have been taking too much of a chance for them and they had no one to counsel them. Negro lawyers back then didn't have that kind of know-how," Mother explained.

The knife grinder who passed with his cart to sharpen utensils; the small grocery store owners; the popcorn man who also sold candy, ice-cold sodas and shaved ice; and the proprietors of a big chicken market nearby—these businesses were owned and operated by white people, mostly Jews. "I used to go to the chicken market with Daddy on Saturday mornings and watch them wring the chickens' necks. Daddy would bring the chickens back and Big Will or Oni would pluck the feathers out. They'd put them in a bucket of hot water out back and pluck them. That was," she shuddered, "a gruesome job."

There were a couple of glaring exceptions to this pattern of white business ownership. First off, once the Carper Casket Company opened its doors in 1932, my grandparents bought all of their coffins from this black-owned business, which exists to this day. Mr. W. C. Maxwell, a Negro photographer, ran St. Louis's premier portrait studio for colored patrons during the first decades of the century. Most of the portrait photos of both sides of my family have "Maxwell" embossed in the lower right-hand corner, along with the street address, 2607 Lawton, which was just across the street from grandparents' house. Equipped with backdrops, draperies, settees, and other paraphernalia, Mr. Maxwell was able to match the setting to any occasion. And finally, my mother gleefully described one concession on wheels that colored people controlled. "They had trucks filled with watermelons, and you could go out there and they would plug a melon for you. They'd take a knife and make a little diamond-shaped plug and pull it out and they'd give it to you to taste to see if that's the melon you wanted. And that was a lot of fun because all of the kids, everybody would be waiting for the watermelon man. And those were usually black men."

Other than the white vendors in the neighborhood, the Hugheses didn't have much to do with Caucasians. "If my parents talked about them, I didn't hear it," she added. Yet my mother did feel bias back in those days because of where she lived. "The Negroes on the west side of Grand Avenue thought they were better than the people east of Grand Avenue. Isn't that ridiculous?" she exclaimed. "As soon as anyone living east of Grand could rub two pennies together, they moved west." Perhaps they fled because of the neighborhood's proximity to Chestnut Street, known as Chestnut Valley, and the alleged bordellos there. Houses on Enright Avenue were beginning to "open up"; that is, whites were moving farther west once Negroes started buying houses close to them. Schoolteachers, postal workers, and doctors took the lead, forming the upper echelon of colored society. Female schoolteachers couldn't marry then because it was against the law. So they saved their money and had an affluent lifestyle. Postal workers had prestige because they worked for the federal government and had job security. Doctors also were assured of an income because they were the only medical game in town for colored. Ninety-nine percent of white physicians would not treat Negroes, and those who did would see them at the private Negro Provident Hospital and not in their offices. Lawyers were way down on the totem pole. They had higher education but didn't have much money. Unfortunately, many blacks hired white attorneys, thinking they would have a better chance in court before a white judge.

My grandmother, however, had no intention of moving west of Grand Avenue; her fantasy home, a sprawling ranch-style house with no stairs to climb, would be on the far south side or somewhere in south St. Louis County.

Overall, 2620 was a congenial household in spite of Oni's mysterious exit. Mother recalled "people coming and going all the time. We would be sitting at the dinner table, and people would come in the back door and up the steps to the living quarters. We had no real fear in those days of unknown people wandering in. Somebody was always delivering or picking up something. And there was always enough food to go around."

While far from lavish or wildly successful, the J. W. Hughes Funeral Home consistently turned a profit. "They could have had a much bigger business but my father just wasn't the sort to get out there and hustle like the other funeral directors did. You had to go to churches, bars, political rallies. Be out there on the streets getting the business. He would hand out his cards and then leave. He just didn't have the personality for it. Lyda Hughes made it work in spite of the fact that she didn't have a husband out there," my mother explained. Paradoxically, Grandpa was elected as president of the Negro undertakers' association at some point during his career.

But my grandfather did have the temperament for looking after his only child. He and my mother would sit together on the front stoop while he read the *Andy Gump* and *Little Orphan Annie* and *Barney Google* comic strips to her until she could on her own; then they would recite them together. On weekends, he would bring home after-supper Chinese food and barbeque from the mostly take-out shops in the neighborhood, just for the two of them. He'd slather her with Vick's salve or goose grease ("whatever that was," my mother always said) whenever she got sick and cover her chest with a red flannel cloth. "Why it had to be red, I'll never know," she added. He'd hoist her over a basin of steaming water to relieve her congestion. They all made her sip sassafras tea in the spring, claiming it cleansed one's blood; poured cod-liver oil down her in the winter for fortification against the cold and spoiled air; and plied her with eggnog during the holidays (sans whiskey). They bathed her bruises and soaked her mosquito bites with witch hazel. "These were all southern remedies," she said.

They never used Grandma's sister Cassie's liniment formula on her, but Mother and I used to laugh whenever we read the recipe: "Take one ½ pt of Red cider vinegar, 3 eggs, crush eggs shell. Ad ½ pt of vinagar. Shake well, then add ½ pt of gasoline. Let stand 24 hours or until it quits foaming. Then it is ready to use. It will turn white or cream. Be sure to let it stand open or it may exsplore [All spellings in the recipe are sic]. You may double it if you want to make more."

John Hughes. Photograph by Maxwell's, ca. 1920.

During the mercilessly hot St. Louis summers, Mother talked about how she would stretch out on her back in a flimsy dress on her bedroom floor to escape the heat. She'd lie there motionless and listen to the trains as they roared in and out of St. Louis, hoping for the day she could board one for parts unknown.

My grandparents were a conventional couple in many ways, and modern in others. Grandma anticipated nearly all of her husband's wishes—so much so that, in silence, he could get whatever he wanted at mealtime. He would merely look a certain way for salt, another for pepper, and she promptly and appropriately responded. She managed the parlor, and he deferred to her good judgment on all major decisions, delivering his routine greeting, "See the madam," to all who arrived at their door on business. He marginally advertised the home's services at churches and bars, dropping off his card and the ubiquitous funeral emblem of the day—the cardboard or straw fan. All of the "homes" printed them and attempted to outdo one another with their mottoes. Worshippers relied on the fans during the summer months and year-round for those who fainted from religious fervor. Besides the name and coordinates, the J. W. Hughes Funeral Home fans sported a "Best in the Business" legend. Each year, my grandparents took separate vacations. Grandpa traveled south to take the baths at Hot Springs, Arkansas, while Grandma went to the first Negro-owned bathhouse in the region, the Waddy in French Lick, Indiana.

At some point, they bought the property next door and turned it into a boardinghouse for Pullman car porters. This sideline paid for some of their expenses during the Depression and leaner years when business tapered off due to greater competition from the larger funeral homes in the more upscale neighborhoods.

My mother finished grade school ahead of time because she started early and skipped a grade. She was a sickly child who suffered from frequent colds during the severe St. Louis winters, and the soft coal only complicated her condition. One of Grandma's sisters, Clara, had left Chicago for San Diego in the twenties. Between the two, they decided that after her first year of high school, Mildred should go west to California to finish. In hindsight, my mother realized that her parents, although mute on the subject, had also wanted to shield her from further insults by her darker-skinned classmates at school, who had called her half white and pulled her auburn banana curls. Clara, a twice-widowed, childless woman, was delighted to host her niece. She

Mildred Hughes (fifth from left) enjoying the snow in Pine Valley Mountains, California, ca. 1932. Aunt Clara Robinson is fourth from left.

was an independent woman with a rambunctious laugh who had assisted her second husband with his general contracting business in Chicago before he died. She did anything she put her mind to, including riding and repairing motorcycles on the side and brewing bathtub gin for her parties during Prohibition. Alone now in San Diego, she created a small catering business.

Mother left St. Louis with the anticipation of warm weather and clear skies. She also abandoned a loving and graceful life in the midst of grit and dirt. She flourished in the San Diego sunshine, and her social life largely revolved around Aunt Clara's and her friends' flurry of get-togethers, weekend hikes in the snowy mountains nearby, and day trips to Tijuana, Mexico. Clara's circle included policemen, chauffeurs, domestics, seamstresses, waiters, and bartenders, who all owned their own homes, worked mostly for white people, and entertained gracefully.

Grandma went to San Diego once while my mother was there. Mommy, however, never returned to St. Louis until after she graduated. Douglas, Nathaniel, and her beloved Big Will all passed away while she was in California, and Grandma embalmed, dressed, adorned, and gave each one of them a proper burial. Thereafter, the J. W. Hughes Funeral Home carried on its work with part-time employees, and the dedication and gaiety that marked the house on Lawton Avenue in the 1920s were no more.

5.

Chicago's South Side

The Promised Land—Almost

WHEN MY MOTHER GRADUATED FROM HIGH SCHOOL IN San Diego, she returned to St. Louis for the summer before she left for college in Chicago, as a mature, self-possessed sixteen-year-old. She would describe her life as a teenager and young adult in the Windy City, where she attended Northwestern University with a handful of other Negroes. She arrived in Evanston, Illinois, each morning on the commuter train from Chicago's fabled South Side. "I lived first with Aunt Sophie. I was crazy about her. I think it was because she was so much like Big Will. Easy and good to be around. She was very religious but she wasn't one to force anything on you," Mother reminisced. "She was an outstanding seamstress. That's how she made her living and how I had so many nice clothes. And also a wonderful cook, just like all those Franklin women were," she exclaimed. "I had to ride the commuter train out to Evanston every morning from the South Side. Sometimes it felt like the train would be blown off its tracks by that wind coming off Lake Michigan. If I didn't have homework to do at the last minute, I'd usually doze off on the way out there." She also stayed with two of her other aunts,

Aunt Clara and Aunt Bert, during her studies. None of them had children and they all wanted a piece of their niece.

Anyone who qualified academically and was able to pay the tuition could attend Chicago's universities and colleges. But the "open door" policy at Northwestern stopped there. My mother and her friends, for instance, couldn't swim in the school's athletic pool. Restaurants in town were, for the most part, off limits. So one of her girlfriend's grandmothers, who ran a boardinghouse in Evanston, would prepare lunch for the colored students each day and charge a pittance. "Evanston was very prejudiced, and we knew just where we could and couldn't go," Mother emphasized.

White racism had been such a huge part of my integration into American society that I was always dumbfounded that my mother never felt it when she grew up, until I really grasped just how different her world had been. Her cocoonlike upbringing had sealed her off, in many ways, from the larger realities of the United States then. "I hadn't been restricted in any way in San Diego. When I came back to St. Louis before going to Chicago, my group and I were having such a good time that summer. You know, parties and things going on, so it never occurred to me, I guess, to even think about the fact that we were on a segregated boat or auditorium," she mused. When she stepped onto Northwestern's campus or ventured outside of Chicago's South Side haven, it finally hit her. "Yes," she admitted, "I guess I could say it was the first time I ever really felt it."

Chicago's racial code was straightforward. Negroes could go downtown to the movie theaters but not into the finer restaurants or the hotels. They could shop in any of the big department stores but had to keep a safe distance from the near North Side's Rush Street, a hotbed of social activity. "We didn't *need* to go over there," my mother emphasized. The sting of racism was lessened by the dazzling nightlife, economic security, and intellectual stimulation offered on the South Side. "It was actually quite a lot of fun being segregated. There was so much to do. There was music everywhere and there were so many swank clubs. The white people came from the north side to the Grand Terrace Café, for instance. That was THE club to go to. Earle "Fatha" Hines ran it, along with the gangsters. We had the Regal Theatre, the Sunset Café, and the Savoy Ballroom, and all the big bands came through town. Some of the best restaurants were on the South Side."

The South Side also had more professionals than St. Louis. They formed a close-knit society and were able to make a lot of money quickly. They bought up large brownstone houses and mansions to reside in, and they invested in other properties throughout the area to rent out. The Vincennes Hotel was the locale for most of the formal dances given by various clubs. It had an ornate ballroom where, in addition to hosting balls and parties, dance instructors gave lessons. South Parkway, Chicago's Negro equivalent of New York's Fifth Avenue, was lined with elegant homes and every kind of shop or business imaginable (barbershops, cleaners, groceries, haberdasheries, beauty shops, art galleries, restaurants, taverns, banks, insurance companies, funeral parlors, and on and on). A majestic thoroughfare (now renamed Dr. Martin Luther King Jr. Drive), it still holds six lanes for traffic. Every Sunday was like Easter, with the locals and out-of-towners dressed up and either driving up and down "South Park" or pushing baby carriages back and forth. For a slightly higher fare, jitney taxis would pull off the main roadway and drop a passenger at his or her front door. The untold clubs, restaurants, theaters, and hotels made jobs plentiful. Some "more enterprising" residents would open up a "policy" wheel, as the illegal lottery game was known in Chicago, and come out millionaires. Policy employed scores

Third from left: Mildred Hughes at a formal dinner dance given by the Modern Gaities Club in the Vincennes Hotel on December 25, 1933, Chicago, Illinois.

and scores of colored Chicagoans. The South Side was energetic, prosperous, and ALIVE!

By the mid-1930s, the Depression finally hit my grandparents, and they had to reduce my mother's educational allowance. She transferred to the less expensive Lewis Institute, but left before graduating. "There were more colored there, so it was easier for us," she said. The only professions readily open to most colored girls were social worker, teacher, or secretary. My mother chose the latter and took a business course at Loyola University Chicago. "I looked into social work because I wanted to do something for people, but it made me too sad. I studied French at Northwestern and used to dream about running off to France, but that was out of the question in those days," she laughed. She eventually landed a job in the offices of the Benjamin Franklin five-and-ten, owned by the Jones brothers, who had come from Mississippi and made a fortune in policy. Before getting this full-time position, however, she had several part-time jobs, including as a cashier in the summer of 1940 at the Chicago Negro Exposition. Organized to celebrate the diamond jubilee of the Emancipation Proclamation, exhibitions from all of the states, some Caribbean islands, and Liberia showcased the accomplishments of Negroes in all fields. "That was very exciting," she remembered, "because it was very well attended and there were people from everywhere."

My mother was amongst the comeliest socialites on the South Side. She and her similarly attractive roommates were pursued by a horde of eligible suitors, most of whom they didn't take very seriously. Before they did marry, they roomed together and borrowed each other's clothing to stretch their meager salaries. They took horseback-riding lessons in Washington Park on Saturday mornings, learned to master English tack (the only riding style in Chicago), and rode the Pancake, a bridle path that encircled the park. Their neighbors would wait outside just for a glimpse of some of Chicago's finest "fillies" as they headed off to the park. They'd return from parties and dates and fill each other's heads for hours with "he said, I said" talk. These women remained my mother's friends for life, and eventually became my surrogate aunts.

The general Negro population began to be more engaged in the nascent civil rights struggle once the United States entered World War II. "We could go to war and get killed but we couldn't do anything else. I began to get very angry about all this," Mother said. "I will never forget the time I took the remains of one of my best friends from Chicago to Henderson, North Carolina. She was only in her twenties when she died from tuberculosis," Mother began. "Once I crossed the Mason-Dixon Line on that train, one of the colored brakemen came to me and said, 'Miss, you have to move up front now. I'll carry your things for you.' I didn't know what he was talking about!" She followed him to a Jim Crow char car with a coal oven. The car came just after the engine, and she was dusted with soot from then on, recalling something she thought she'd left behind on the windowsills at 2620 Lawton Avenue. "I remember sitting next to a young man who had a college degree. He was a lieutenant in the army, with his gold bars on his uniform. He had just graduated from Officer Training School and was going home for a visit. We talked about the hypocrisy of it all. That made quite an impression on me. I was furious but I didn't know what to do. You see, we didn't have the connections then. But there was the *Chicago Defender* and the *Pittsburgh Courier.* These newspapers were outspoken even though I wasn't interested in politics, really, until I came back to St. Louis and met your father," she confessed.

It was becoming more and more apparent to her that behind Chicago's magnetic façade, there were many restrictions. "Jobs for Negro girls were really very limited when I think about it," Mother admitted. Once she saw through the veneer, she felt that it was time for her to move back to California, where she had experienced more freedom than anywhere else. She also missed its sunny climate. One of her dearest friends had been encouraging her to come back to the West Coast. "She kept telling me there were good jobs to be had for colored. I thought I wanted to be a career girl."

Before she left, however, she began visiting St. Louis. Grandma had been ill, and my mother hoped to spruce up and modernize her parents' faltering undertaking business before she went so far away from them. Their funeral home had become overshadowed by other Negro parlors. These, begun as modestly as my grandparents', had mostly moved west and north into more upscale buildings. Storefront churches had grown into full-scale religious institutions able to accommodate larger funerals and, at some, hundreds of mourners. The wakes, however, still took place at an undertaking establishment the night before. But Lawton Avenue had changed drastically in the intervening years, and the neighborhood was much less inviting. Some of the rowdiness east of Jefferson had crept west. My grandparents had both slowed down and were resistant to any of the improvements Mommy suggested. The rooming house next door supplemented their income while the funeral business took a back seat. Grandma's fantasy of moving to a "ranch-style home on the far south side" remained just that.

Above all and for the first time in my mother's life, she encountered institutional racism wherever she turned. Only Fred Harvey's restaurant and the streetcars were integrated in the early 1940s. There were random incidents of violence on the cars (with the conductors' complicity) when Negroes refused to ride in the back. "I never rode the streetcars because I still had a car and driver at my disposal. And St. Louis had a nice social life. People entertained a lot in their homes because they couldn't go any place else. There was Jordan Chambers's Club Riviera and the Club Plantation, which was owned by Jews. Cab [Calloway] played there a few times. We just had no nice places to go to. There were a few restaurants, three or four little clubs, and a lot of Negro taverns."

She had no idea of what was in store for her when she met my father, who was recently divorced and one of the most eligible

VISITED BY MOTHER

MISS MILDRED HUGHES

Comely Chicago socialite who was | visit from her mother, Mrs. John
plenty surprised recently by a | W. Hughes, St. Louis business
| mona.—Photo by Young St. Louis.

Mildred Hughes article in Chicago Defender, *April 2, 1938.*
Copyright Chicago Defender.

bachelors in town. "When I came to St. Louis to visit from Chicago in the '30s, people were talking about what he was doing. I just heard that he was a well-known lawyer and a great orator and one of the first Negro Democrats in town. I wasn't interested in politics when I visited St. Louis then. It wasn't until the '40s when I came back—we had a date and we went to Herculaneum for a rally and that was the first time I was really impressed with him. It was on the disparity of wages between black and white teachers. Local people had gotten together and wanted him to help them. He was a dynamic speaker and it didn't take too long before he left an impression on everybody he met. He definitely opened my eyes to a lot of things."

Virtually every redcap at Union Station got to know my father during the year that my parents courted. "She's coming on the 8:25 tonight from Chicago. Right, Lawyer Grant?" they'd ask him. "You betcha," he might answer, or "No, she'll be in on the 8:45 from Detroit. She's been visiting some friends there," he might say. They surprised everyone by eloping in Kansas City on September 18, 1944, during one of Daddy's speaking engagements. He was still building his legal practice and didn't have much money, so they moved into the third floor of my grandparents' funeral home. "Mama was wild about Dave," my mother always told me, but she wasn't enamored enough to change her political affiliation. Grandma was pleased when they wed, but no amount of his razzing could make her budge from the Republican Party.

"When Dave and I were living there until we moved to Arsenal Street, they really didn't have much business. I do remember that she was very happy when she had a $900 funeral. That was a lot of money then for a funeral. Can you imagine? $900! She still embalmed and they had wakes, but it wasn't like before," my mother remembered. "I never stayed around when she had a wake. I don't know. Maybe what I didn't feel as a child began to bother me. I didn't want to be around dead people. It made me too sad. I'd always go out."

6.

RIDING A DIFFERENT KIND
OF CURRENT

Political Activism in the 1930s and 1940s

HEN MY PARENTS MARRIED, MY FATHER'S LIFE HAD BEEN
full of nonstop political wrangling for nearly fifteen
years. By the time my brother and I were old enough to understand his "stories," he was in his early fifties and had stepped
somewhat out of the limelight. So he loved reliving his exploits
by telling us about St. Louis politics when he was in the thick
of it. He especially liked telling us about the controversy he and
others provoked when they encouraged blacks to abandon Abraham Lincoln's Republican Party and embrace the Democrats, a
party with a broad swath of diehard Southern segregationists at
the time.

It all started when he came back to St. Louis after graduating
from Howard University Law School in 1930, where he'd gotten
more than just legal training. "Charles Houston was a teacher and
the vice dean and he was a giant of a man. He wanted to graduate social activists and he instilled that spirit into us from the
moment we entered Howard," Daddy always told me.

My father passed the bar exam on the first go-round and
opened an office with a classmate in downtown St. Louis. Yet

when he hung out his shingle the very first day, he used to tell us, "Well I said to myself, I hope nobody comes through that door wanting a lawyer 'cause I won't know what to do!" He felt that law school didn't teach one how to practice the law. "A lot of white boys go into law firms as clerks where they learn what to do. We didn't have that sort of a thing. Hence, you had to learn after you got out," he always said. So he and his friend sat there together teaching themselves and each other how to represent clients. Before long, Daddy involved himself in another kind of business. He looked around and saw a city held captive by the Republican Party.

"When I came home, I went through the dusty records of the election returns . . . and I knew generally the areas in which Negroes lived. And I discovered that it was their vote that was keeping the Republican Party in power." Moreover, he saw that rewards for their loyalty were few, despite the best efforts of the Citizens' Liberty League, a colored Republican organization founded in the early 1900s. It had persistently tried to get its candidates elected (with limited success) but was duped repeatedly by the Republican bosses. Those who did get jobs received the filthiest employment—mopping floors and carrying slop buckets with the mules. A colored assistant city counselor in the Law Department held the only valid white-collar job. Several other appointees worked in the so-called County Offices but at times were required to do double duty as gardeners and butlers in their bosses' homes. "I was incensed at what Negroes had received in return for what they had given and I was determined to expose it," he said.

So he began what would become a lifelong affiliation with the Democratic Party, but not out of any admiration for it. He and other Negro activists were beginning to see how much the Republicans had taken their votes for granted. They also felt that the Republicans had sold them out with the Compromise of 1877. In order to retain the White House in a contested race, the Republicans agreed to pull out federal troops from Southern states. This move effectively destroyed Reconstruction and cleared the way for the rise of Jim Crow laws throughout the South and bordering states, including Missouri.

To get fully on board with the Democrats, Daddy knew whom he had to meet. In 1928, Joseph L. McLemore, a Negro attorney, had posed the first significant challenge to the Republicans in St. Louis. Running as a black Democrat from the Twelfth Congressional District, he opposed the white incumbent, Leonidas C. Dyer. McLemore ran well but lost. Before 1928, at times the Democrats wouldn't even bother to run a candidate. If any colored Republicans jumped into the primary race, they would split up the vote, thereby assuring Dyer's return to Congress. "It was said that the Republicans would tell their Democrat opponents, 'I'll spot you 25,000 votes and still beat you,' AND THEY COULD!" my father bellowed.

In 1931, before he leapt into ward politics with McLemore and other freshly minted Democrats, he attacked white businesses. He organized the first Negro economic boycott the city had ever seen. Woolworth's had just opened a five-and-dime store in a solidly Negro neighborhood—and it had no intention of hiring any of the black population it served. White clerks would fill every post. My father joined with other colored professionals to form the Neighborhood Improvement Association. They demanded that the store hire black clerks. "We've got colored janitors, so why are you complaining?" was their reply. So the Negro leaders soon strung a picket line across the entrance to the store. The *St. Louis Argus,* a Negro newspaper, circulated fifty thousand handbills, and colored St. Louis soon learned of this new movement. People on the picket line were paid $4 a week. They were arrested and accused of being Communists. Jordan "Pops" Chambers, a colored Republican committeeman, signed the bail bonds, and my father represented the pickets in court, gratis. No one was ever convicted, and once released, they returned to the picket line. Negro doctors and businessmen had agreed to underwrite the costs of the picket line, but the Depression was tattering the heels of even the fanciest shoes in town—and the doctors could not deliver on their promise. Some were unable to contribute the $1 per week that they had pledged. My father literally paid one man with the shirt off his back—"one fellow was about my size, so I paid him by giving him some of my clothes," he said. Woolworth's first hired one colored woman who sold ice cream in the doorway and eventually two or three clerks inside the store. This achievement remained one of my father's proudest accomplishments. He was barely twenty-eight years old.

Inspired by this success, he helped organize the Colored Clerks' Circle, which began targeting a string of stores along Easton Avenue for the same reason—only white clerks for black customers. The *St. Louis American,* another Negro newspaper, invented a "Don't Spend Where You Can't Work" slogan in response to this campaign. Daddy served as the Circle's legal counsel free of charge. Through picketing, they succeeded in securing hundreds of jobs for Negroes from 1932 to 1937 in these stores. Some of the colored clerks benefited by more than just getting a paycheck. Able to see the material rewards of owning even a small business, some sought to open stores of their own.

"The next year, McLemore and I and some of the new Democrats started what we called the Negro Central Democratic Organization. We had to name it that to distinguish ourselves from the white Democratic committeemen who represented the colored wards," he explained. These whites were believed to reside comfortably within the deep and expensively lined pockets of the wards' Republicans.

Protesters with the Colored Clerks' Circle, ca. 1932. Vivian Grant is in the middle with no sign. Western Historical Manuscript Collection.

"Now mind you, Negroes had been brainwashed to believe that the Republican Party was birthed and born and organized and came into being for the *sole* purpose of freeing the slaves, which, of course, was untrue." My father firmly believed this and became unwavering whenever the topic came up. So, among other things, these upstarts went about the difficult task of deprogramming generations of colored people who had tethered themselves to the GOP because of their belief that Abraham Lincoln saved the race by his wholesale abolition of slavery. They hit hard and as far below the belt as they could, first by demythologizing America's untouchable sixteenth president and the revered Civil War.

Daddy goaded his colored brothers, as early as 1930 when he first began to try to unbrainwash them, by saying "that any Negro who thought that 600,000 white people decided to kill each other in order to free him—that they were crazy." He personally believed that the Civil War was fought to "free labor." My head still spins when I think about how he drummed his theory into me and how long it took me to grasp it. I remember telling my freshman high school citizenship class, "My father said that Lincoln didn't free the slaves." I didn't say too much more than that because I didn't understand any more than that at the time. My teacher didn't dispute what I said. She knew who my father was. She just looked bewildered and changed the subject.

In short, he'd first tell me about the Dred Scott case, which began its journey through the courts in St. Louis in 1848 and ended up in the U.S. Supreme Court. Scott was a slave. Backed by abolitionists, he petitioned for his and his wife's freedom, claiming they were so entitled because they had both lived long enough in states and territories where slavery was illegal. The high court ultimately ruled in 1857 that no person of African descent could be a citizen of the United States because the writers of the Constitution never intended such people to be. Writing for the majority, the chief justice, himself a Maryland slave owner, stated that they "had no rights which the white man was bound to respect." In effect, they were mere property and had no standing in a court of law. My father told me that when he studied constitutional law at Howard, his professor claimed that there was evidence that the justices had colluded, vowing to settle the question of slavery—for good, for once and for all. "And they DID," he stressed, "until the Civil War."

"So with the Dred Scott decision," he concluded, "it was clear that this country was going to become a slavocracy. Corporations in the North, manufacturing and so on, were just beginning. The only thing a corporation cares about is profit. So it was easy to see that there were these two diametrically opposed economic systems: one based on paid wages at the North, the other on free slave labor at the South—that these two systems could not compete in a single economy and it wouldn't take a genius to know that it would not be long before the slave system would take over and the time would come when there would be no job that a white man could get unless he sold himself into slavery. There was no authority higher than the United States Supreme Court to reverse the Dred Scott decision, and that's what actually led to the Civil War, which had to be fought in order to halt this system," he deduced. In the 1850s, some had called it a wanton Slave Power movement that swept the land. Many Civil War theories contradict my father's theory, but he was so firmly rooted in it that nothing could change his mind. His argument was also born out of a distrust of white men's motives; he couldn't accept that they would wage a war on behalf of slaves alone.

He and his cronies also hammered away at President Lincoln's two executive orders on slavery, better known as the Emancipation Proclamation. "I'm always amused at blacks celebrating the Emancipation Proclamation, which is nothing but a hoax. It never freed a single slave who could be freed," he believed. "It couldn't free anyone because it only applied to those states in rebellion. All you got to do is read it!"

With their blasphemous talk, these new Democrats were viewed as impertinent renegades. "In fact, it was worse in 1930 to be black and a Democrat than it is today to be a card-carrying Communist. Now this is a fact. . . . I experienced it," he noted.

"Turning our backs on the Great Emancipator and throwing our lot with the likes of white Southern Democrats. Well, you can imagine how we were looked at."

But he and his group needed more than rhetoric to convince an electorate to join their ranks, so they tackled inadequate health care for Negroes. Beginning at the turn of the twentieth century, colored voters started vocally opposing having their tax dollars finance hospitals where only white medical workers could be trained. Provident Hospital, which opened in 1894 and was run privately by Negro physicians for their patients, brought St. Louis its first "training" facility of any sort for Negro medical workers when its nursing school opened in 1899. Originally housed two blocks from my mother's home in a three-story brownstone, not unlike the houses where both of my parents were reared, the facility was small and only for patients who could pay. Later known as People's Hospital, it eventually moved into the larger building where I was born.

While my father was still in high school, Negro doctors and businessmen began pressuring city authorities to do something. City officials began to pay attention as the pool of potential colored voters mushroomed, seeing a 69 percent increase in Negro residents from 1910 to 1920. In 1918, the city allotted enough funds to take possession of the vacant former Barnes Medical College Building, which was never meant to serve as a hospital. It was turned into a 177-bed health care facility for Negroes and opened in 1919. Named City Hospital No. 2 to distinguish it from the segregated City Hospital, the label's implications infuriated colored physicians. Some say it was already overcrowded and obsolete from day one.

The physicians and an attorney named Homer G. Phillips then started another campaign, aimed at getting a brand-new

City Hospital No. 2, ca. 1920. Missouri History Museum.

*Homer G. Phillips Hospital, 2000 North Whittier Street. Photograph by
W. C. Persons, 1938. Missouri History Museum.*

facility built with some of the money allocated by a 1922 bond issue for capital improvements. Phillips had taken the lead in lobbying against a municipal plan to build a ward for colored at the City Hospital (before the Barnes Medical College Building was funded), feeling that it would be devoid of training opportunities for Negro doctors. He warned, more suspiciously, that it might give white doctors a means to "experiment" on colored patients. In a referendum on the bond issue the next year, a line item was inserted that called for the construction of a major Negro teaching hospital on the city's north side. The entire bond docket was passed with the votes from the city's colored wards and through a coalition of downtown elites and Progressive activists in the Democratic Party. Republicans still ruled city hall, and the colored community still waited for the first brick to be laid. Victor Miller, mayor at the time, "was out of his head," according to my father. "Miller said he was so tired of hearing about this nigger hospital that he didn't give a damn if they built it in the Mississippi River. Now this was said," my father emphasized.

In the meantime, some of the bond's funds did go for a hospital—to treat monkeys at the zoo. And some of it went toward maintaining City Hospital No. 2. By the early 1930s, the situation there was catastrophic; it housed a sweeping mix of hundreds of men, women, and children, all jumbled up together. In spots, two beds were tied together at night in order to sleep three or more patients.

Daddy loved telling me about his 3:00 a.m. "raid" on the hospital. "We couldn't take the people to the hospital, so we decided to take the hospital to the people." So he, a photographer, and three others bullied their way into City Hospital No. 2 and took one picture after the other. They put together a slide show and carried it throughout the Negro wards for the voters to see. Dr. Oral McClellan, one of the night raiders at the hospital, added shots from the zoo to his presentation to chilling effect. "He went out to the zoo and got pictures of the monkey hospital, which was a beautiful thing. He said that since he had to be born in St. Louis, he was just sorry that God didn't make him a monkey. So if he got sick, he could get some decent hospital care," my father recounted. Furthermore, an intern had been electrocuted at the hospital in 1930 as he x-rayed a patient's chest using a defective machine with exposed high-tension wires. So there was plenty to criticize. It would be 1937 before a hospital for Negroes would open.

"We began in 1932. Mind you, that was when the Depression was at its depths. Roosevelt was elected president. Soup lines and the apple sellers and well, you know what the Depression was—banks failing and everything else, and all of it, of course, was blamed on the Republican administration," Daddy said. President Herbert Hoover's inept handling of the Depression added to their ammunition to fight the Republicans. Shantytowns, mockingly nicknamed "Hoovervilles," cropped up all over the United States for those who had no place to live after the 1929 stock market crash. St. Louis had many, strung together for miles along the banks of the Mississippi River. The first appeared in 1929, and the final one was dismantled by the Works Project Administration in 1936; they were the largest and longest lasting in the United States. Continual reminders of the Republican administration's failure to confront the ills caused by the Depression, they were also one of the few St. Louis communities where colored and whites lived side by side. Tenants throughout the country soon invented a glossary for almost everything they used and attached the president's name to most of them: a Hoover flag was an empty pocket turned inside out; Hoover leather was cardboard that sub

Hooverville on the St. Louis riverfront, March 6, 1934. Photograph by Isaac Sievers, Sievers Studio Collection, Missouri History Museum.

stituted for a shoe sole; and a Hoover wagon was a horse-drawn automobile since the owner couldn't afford gasoline.

My father and his colleagues now had to ensure that St. Louis would join the changing political tide by getting the first Democratic mayor elected in almost a quarter of a century. Jordan Chambers switched sides during the campaign and brought along his Cooperative Civic Association, a potent political organization that could deliver votes. His participation as a Democrat until his death in 1962 would be vital to the party's success in St. Louis.

Chambers wore many hats throughout his life, including the ten-gallon ones he handsomely sported in later years. His "day" jobs were varied: funeral parlor owner and director, constable, Nineteenth Ward committeeman, and nightclub proprietor. It was even said that he and my father convinced Harry Truman, when running for president in 1948, to address a crowd of black constituents from on top of a crate in the back of Chambers's funeral parlor! Above all and evident early on, he was the textbook grassroots organizer and the closest thing to a Negro political boss that St. Louis had ever seen. He dropped out of Sumner High School to get married, worked as a railway car cleaner, and quickly noted the difference between wages for whites and colored. So he wrote to the American Federation of Labor president for information on how to set up a union. He and about ten other men formed the Railway Coach Cleaners Union No. 16088. From 1918 to 1923, when Chambers served as its business agent, it had a membership of 1,100. My father held him in the highest regard and served as his counsel. They had first met at Sumner High School. "A very wise man. A very firm man, and a farseeing fellow who had the respect of the entire political family of St. Louis, principally because he kept his word at all times." Any candidate who received Chambers's endorsement could count on it.

Although he died while I was in elementary school, I have a vivid recollection of him. He had abandoned his legendary foulard adorned with an eye-popping diamond stickpin by then, and he looked like a black Wyatt Earp to me. He often wore a string tie, cowboy boots, and a knee-length waistcoat with his sidearm, at times, detectable, and he always chomped on a cigar as thick as a handlebar. He drove a spotless Cadillac around town, and I heard about the horses he rode on his farm in the Ozarks. He may have gotten cowboy fever from having driven a team of horses for the city as one of his first jobs after he left Sumner. More likely, his enduring passion for the ponies started as a child. His father worked on a stock farm, and Jordan would tag along just to gaze at the horses. He had a great big laugh and was always kind to me whenever I saw him. Even as a child, I sensed his strength but also his solitude.

My mother remembered him as "a gentleman, although he was known for his rough, tough language and his demeanor sometimes was, maybe, abrasive, especially to white people. Jordan never, ever showed any fear—never," she emphasized.

He surrounded himself with such people as Fred Weathers, a former college professor and top-of-the-class Wharton Busi-

Elmer Mosee (administrator of People's Hospital and early black Democrat), Jordan Chambers, and David M. Grant, ca. 1944.

ness School graduate; my father; and other lawyers. They gave him ideas, and he had the shrewdness and political muscle to give them shape and make them work. Chambers demanded that his on-the-ground staffers, the precinct captains, tell him anything that affected the people in his ward—every ailment or predicament. And he fixed it with a job or a loan or a doctor's appointment, thereby binding "his people" to him. White politicians came to Chambers for a vote count, knowing he would deliver. With Chambers and his Cooperative Civic Association now on board, the Democrats took on a full head of steam.

As my father became more involved in local Democratic politics, he soon learned that besides being considered a turncoat, joining the party carried certain personal risks. "Most of the Democratic leaders ran questionable houses and gambling games down on the levee; in other words, the half-world. I used to go down there because I lived out on Enright Avenue and I didn't expect them to come out to where I was," he told me. Some of my father's clients also patronized these hangouts, which attracted the cops on a regular basis. Back then, there were two contradictory laws on the books: one said that no one could be held for one minute unless there was a reason, and the other said that if anybody was held for twenty hours without being charged, the detainee had to be released. This absurdity allowed the police a convenient way to harass colored people, literally for days if they wanted. After twenty hours elapsed and no charge was placed, the person would be released to a corner where another cop would be waiting to take him to another district for yet another twenty-hour "holding" period. "They didn't have to put a charge; they didn't have to suspect you of anything, just arrest you for investigation. And they would hold you twenty hours. So really," Daddy remarked, "sometimes you couldn't find out where your client was."

He oftentimes would get swooped up in one of the cops' raids when strategizing with his Democratic colleagues on the levee in the early 1930s. The incident he most frequently told me about took place in a little bar that sold moonshine. "Well, they [a couple of cops] walked in and made an announcement, 'All you black SOBs line up against the wall over there!' I didn't move, and pretty soon a cop came over and said, 'Did you hear what I said?' and I said, 'Yes, I heard you said something about some black SOBs; you weren't talking to me.' The cop looked at me and said, 'Oh! You're a smart black SOB.'" My father got such a kick out of this story that he couldn't even get to the punch line without laughing through it.

Inevitably, he would be taken to the central district lockup and booked without any charge attached. I hated to think about my father sitting in jail when he told me these stories, but he recounted them in such a way that I finally understood that he didn't mind it. Besides, he usually got to chew out some cop by the time he was released. Whenever Daddy was taken to the lockup, he would be questioned about what he did for a living. "I am a lawyer and that would disturb them a little bit," he'd say. But it didn't prevent them from arresting him. Then the police would search for one of the eight or nine Negro cops on the force at the time to confirm his profession. "I knew every one of them, and they all knew me," he added. In the meantime, his colored cell mates were always stumped. "Mr. Grant, you don't have to be in here with us. Why don't you tell them WHO you are?" He'd always answer, "I tried to explain that I was trying to help them, but they couldn't see it."

After a half hour or so, one of the Negro cops would appear and identify my dad. They'd let him out of the cell in a flash but stop him before he could leave the building. "They'd give me the side arm treatment. You know, take me aside. Then they'd begin to tell me what a good cop this was, the one who'd just got through calling me those names and locking me up for nothing. And I'd listen to them and say, 'Well, that may be true, but he's going to have to write a report because I'm going to find out why he brought me up here, and I had done nothing, and he had no right to do it. So you can say he's fine and all that, but to me he's just an overbearing cop and I'm going to write him up.'" In those days, the police suspected any Negro who didn't look humble or defeated, or whose "eyes weren't right," as my father put it. Whenever Daddy talked about the "rather impressive police record—oh, possibly ten or twelve" detentions that he acquired during the early 1930s, I always noticed a certain glint in his eyes. That's when I realized just how much his escapades amused him. "The only thing I used to get frightened about was being slugged on the way up, but I never was. Maybe because I talked my way out of it and maybe it was because of the general manner I had that they were, maybe, a little scared of me," he explained.

Maybe that was also because my father's reputation as a real "swinger" preceded him. He didn't acquire it from hanging out in singles' bars; he was known as one who was quick to throw a punch when confronted with any racial humiliation. More than one of his friends told me that, at least once, he knocked out a white man on a streetcar who called him a nigger. He never dwelled on his scuffles when talking with me but did eventually disclose that a good deal of his arrest record was also for "fighting." He added, however, that his mother's clairvoyant intervention in Detroit as he was about to get a gun and go after the white man who almost yanked his eye out, as well as realizing that the legal sword was more lethal and lasting than a wallop, helped him calm down.

The determination of my father and his cohorts helped put the Democrats back in charge of city hall after a twenty-four year hiatus, when Bernard F. Dickmann was sworn in as mayor in 1933. "He was elected because we had been able to win over some of the black folks," Daddy commented. The City had broken ground for the new colored hospital in 1932 while Republicans were still in office but, shortly thereafter, the work stopped. As soon as Dickmann became mayor, construction began again. When the cornerstone was laid in 1933, he presided, along with a host of reporters and photographers, and thereby cemented his claim to delivering on his campaign promise to build a hospital for poor Negro St. Louisans. When it was dedicated on February 22, 1937, the governor, the senior Missouri U.S. senator, a member of Congress, and the U.S. secretary of the interior participated. It opened four months later and, with a 685-bed capacity, became the largest municipally operated general hospital for colored patients in the world.

Daddy gave it a less distinguished title. "They built what I claimed was the biggest Jim Crow institution in the world. . . . Here is where you, even though you hated Jim Crow, you had to embrace it," my father explained. Almost instantaneously, Homer G. Phillips Hospital became a premier training ground for Negro MDs, with thousands of aspiring physicians receiving their post–medical school education during its existence. Interns and residents fought for internships and residencies at "Homer G.," as it was called. Along with the old Freedman's Hospital at Howard University's Medical School in Washington, D.C., and the Meharry Medical College and Hospital in Nashville, this St. Louis landmark stood as a beacon for colored physicians for decades. With a few exceptions, such as Provident Hospital in Chicago and Harlem Hospital in New York City, Negro medi-

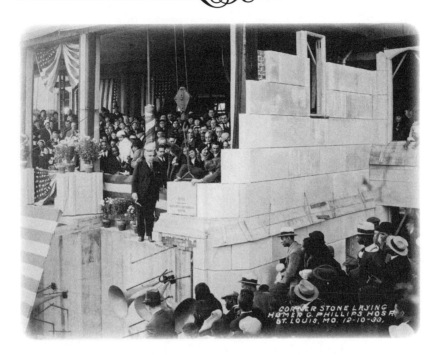

Mayor Bernard F. Dickmann, with trowel, at cornerstone laying for Homer G. Phillips Hospital, December 10, 1933. Photograph by Richard Moore, Missouri History Museum.

cal school graduates could not train anywhere else. The few who were admitted at other institutions were marginalized and mostly miserable.

As a reward for my father's obstinate crusade as a Negro Democrat, he was named assistant city counselor in the city's Condemnation Division, thus beginning his first association with city hall that would last just shy of a decade. The sole Democrat in the office, he worked on the exercise of eminent domain, that is, the condemning of land for public use. At that time, the office was in charge of making the express highway happen and with widening the thoroughfares. "In those days, I was pretty uppish. We had these long blueprints that might have been fifteen feet long. He [his boss] took me over to a table and he showed me how to fold one of these blueprints so it would fit into a petition. Well, I said to him, 'I see where my legal training was inadequate.' He asked me what I meant. 'I didn't get a course in map folding.' So he said that somebody has to do it, and he walked on away from me."

Besides folding maps, however, by 1936 he became the "leading Negro Democrat in St. Louis and patronage dispenser for the party," according to the *New York Herald Tribune.* A bit of an overstatement because Jordan Chambers was the biggest boss behind handing out jobs in those days. But my mother said that "Jordan and Dave and the others worked on deciding which man to endorse. White men. And the white politicians were scared of him [Chambers]; he had just that much power. They had to come to him." She then reiterated my father's exact words: "He was a very wise man. He could look at a politician and tear him to pieces. He'd shake his head and say, 'No, he ain't the one.' And he was always right. I am sure that he had some disasters but I don't know about them." Directly and indirectly, Daddy did have his hand in patronage. He was in on who ran, and if the man won, he was there at Jordan's table to distribute the spoils because he had recommended someone who was qualified, my mother concluded.

The New York paper, however, correctly described my father's speaking abilities: "Only 34 years old, with a booming oratorical voice, Grant has convinced the white Democrats that the Negroes are not playing possum with the party [and] that he has also persuaded many Negroes to join it." Daddy used to tell me that he was "quite an orator in his day," but never elaborated beyond that. I only wished I could have heard him speak before thousands of spectators. I witnessed him hold forth in a courtroom on a few occasions, and he was, in my mind, riveting. People said the full range of his voice was only evident before an audience—the bigger, the better. Instead, I had to rely on what others said, including U.S. Senator Tom Eagleton, who once used a superlative in describing my father's speaking skills to me. "Best," "most dynamic," "most compelling," I can't remember the exact words, but he was clearly impressed.

Daddy did not practice law for the city per se during those years. "The black city attorneys did not appear in court," he explained to me. This was a sore point that would plague him once he worked again as a full-time lawyer. Negro lawyers would have a "hell of a time" getting clients since judges looked more favorably on black defendants who were represented by white attorneys. In any event, he learned a lot about what prosecuting attorneys did. And he campaigned relentlessly for the Democrats and against the unjust. In 1938, the U.S. Supreme Court ruled that the University of Missouri would either have to admit Negroes to its law school or establish a separate (Jim Crow) facility to train lawyers. Missouri chose the latter route and established the Lincoln University Law School in the Poro College Building (a beauty school) on the north side. Daddy's arrest record got another notch when the school opened. Besides leading a picket line in front of the school ("Poro Jim Crow Law School Must Go," read one of the placards), he shuttled others to the site in his car. After a heated exchange with the cops, they arrested him for blocking traffic. "I later learned that the police had been told, 'Just call him "boy" and he'll give you grounds to lock him up,' which they did, and I gave them reason," he chuckled. "Lincoln turned out some fine attorneys who did very well," he added, "but I was just dead set against segregated education, knowing that separate was rarely equal. A building doesn't make a law school. Faculty and resources do."

David M. Grant, 1937.

Daddy stayed in the City Counselor's Office from the summer of 1933 until January 1941 when Thomas Hennings, the newly elected Democratic circuit attorney, appointed him as one of his assistants. That year, the Democrats lost the mayor's office and a goodly number of Board of Aldermen seats, mostly because of the coal issue. Dickmann laid claim to brightening up St. Louis's skies by pushing an ordinance that required residents who used coal to switch from the bituminous variety to the anthracitic. The brunt of this change fell on the poor and mostly colored electorate who still relied heavily on "soft" coal; anthracite cost more than double per ton. After this smashing defeat, Jordan Chambers quipped, "We got overconfident and you can never do that in politics."

Daddy's story about how he got booted out of this job was one of his favorites and one of mine. He would leave this salaried position after thirteen months without another one waiting, with virtually nothing in his savings account, and with his first marriage in shambles. I always used to think about what happened to him that year whenever I had troubles of my own, seeing them quickly evaporate when compared with what he faced. Tom Hennings, a man my father greatly admired, soon left the job for the navy, and Henry G. Morris became acting office chief. My father was the first Negro attorney in sixteen years to join this office. "I was the library man and it was good training, but Morris never did like me. My eyes were never right," Daddy laughed.

In late January 1942, a gang of vigilantes lynched a colored man in Sikeston, Missouri, sealing Daddy's future for years. His outrage at and subsequent association with the murder worsened his relationship with his boss. He told Morris of his decision to join a committee and head to the state capital to petition the governor to declare martial law in Sikeston. The group, including members of the National Association for the Advancement

Editorial cartoon: "Not in Poland, Not in conquered China, But Right in Missouri." St. Louis Star-Times, *January 27, 1942, p. 10. Reprinted with permission of the* St. Louis Post-Dispatch, *copyright 1942.*

of Colored People (NAACP), believed that Sikeston's prosecuting attorney, David E. Blanton, was biased.

The incident had gained national notoriety, occurring so shortly after the bombing of Pearl Harbor; the Japanese even used the lynching in its anti-American propaganda campaign. The details of the case were gruesome: Cleo Wright, a colored oil mill worker, had broken into a house and repeatedly stabbed one of its residents, a white woman and a soldier's wife. Caught by the police, he knifed a marshal while in custody and, in turn, was shot four times and beaten with a revolver. Wright eventually was moved to city hall, laid in an unguarded area, and left to die while a gang of hoodlums gathered in front of the building. The prosecuting attorney tried to dissuade them—unsuccessfully. They kidnapped Wright, tied his legs to a car bumper, and dragged him down the main avenue and through the heart of the Negro community on a Sunday morning as churches were letting out. "The State Highway Patrol rode ahead of the car, telling Negroes to get off the street, get off the sidewalk. Instead of trying to protect that man, that's the way they performed," as Daddy described it to me. In Blanton's own words, he admitted, "One of the troopers and I went out to Sunset [the Negro part of Sikeston] to warn people to stay inside." At some point, the gang cut Wright loose, poured five gallons of gasoline on him, and lit a match. Initially, Blanton said he could recognize none of the vigilantes.

My father said that Morris grew sarcastic as they waged a verbal battle over Daddy's joining the group headed to the state capital. "Are you so great that it [the Jefferson City trip] can't succeed without you? Why do YOU have to go?" my father remembered Morris saying. He left the office with no clear directive from his boss and went to Jefferson City. When he returned to work, Mayor William Dee Becker told him to submit his resignation and Daddy demanded that he put his reasons in writing, but Becker refused. "If you think the choice between the respect of 70,000 St. Louis Negroes and a $4,200 job was hard to make, you've got another think coming," he recalled saying to the newspapers.

So he decided to take up residence on the other side of the courtroom and became a defense attorney. To his great surprise, he pulled in over $800 in his first month on his own, almost doubling what his salary had been. Several years later, he had one more opportunity to "thank" another white man for forcing him out of a job, evoking the episode with Mr. Hart. After Hennings returned from the war and resumed his position, my father paid him a visit. With Henry Morris present, Daddy toasted his former boss: "Tom, Henry thinks I have animosity against him, but he's my greatest benefactor because I didn't know what was out there to be had. I'd become wage addicted. When I was thrown out, I had to get out into the practice and I have Henry to thank for opening the door to my freedom and liberty, also to my economic advantage." My parents would marry in 1944 and Daddy would become a father eleven months later, something he thought would never happen. He and his first wife, although married for eleven years, wanted but never had children. As I said, his comeback boosted my morale whenever I had my own setbacks.

Besides the monetary rewards, his departure from city hall gave him full liberty to plunge more deeply into the fight for civil rights. Almost immediately, he led the battle to equalize Negro teachers' salaries with those of whites in rural Missouri. Both the local branch of the NAACP and the Missouri State Association of Negro Teachers engaged him to study the issue.

In the late 1930s, Thurgood Marshall, then special counsel to the NAACP in New York, had won a case that forced the state of Maryland to pay Negro teachers the same as whites. My father knew Marshall when they served together on the NAACP Legal Redress Committee in the late 1930s, so he began writing to him. Daddy also contacted Walter White, NAACP executive secretary, and asked that Marshall come to St. Louis to address a mass rally organized by the Negro teachers' association on January 31, 1943. Marshall attended and described his experiences as counsel in Maryland and other states where suits had been won or were filed and pending. His appearance kicked off a fundraising campaign that quickly exceeded its goal. Contributions poured in from throughout the state; St. Louis teachers who did not suffer from wage disparities donated more than half of the total amount collected.

Marshall's connection did not stop that night. He came to Missouri several times in the following months to meet with school authorities and, ultimately, join Daddy as co-counsel for six teachers from the Festus, Missouri, school district who filed a lawsuit. The suit was officially filed in June, but they didn't have to go to court. The Festus School Board relented and adopted a new equal salary policy in August. When notified, Daddy sent a special delivery, handwritten letter to Marshall asking him if he wanted to come to Missouri "to be in on the kill" for the forthcoming announcement. Following official notification by the board, the presiding federal judge signed a court order and consent degree on August 14, which read in part: "The official policy and acts of the defendants . . . in so far as such differentials were predicated on race or color, are unlawful, unconstitutional and are in violation of the Fourteenth Amendment."

The six teachers got an average salary increase of $320 per year. The press talked about the precedent-setting nature of the order and predicted that the other 150 school districts in Missouri could be affected, but little happened. It took many years and more battles before an across-the-board change. Win one, lose one, and later win or lose another. "And that's the way she goes."

Later in 1943, the NAACP took aim at integrating department store lunch counters downtown. By spring 1944, frustrated with the stores' lack of response to their letters, a group of women, led by Mrs. Pearl Maddox, organized the Citizens' Civil Rights

Committee (CCRC) and started "sitting in." These were some of the first such actions in the United States. They expanded membership beyond the NAACP and invited some of their white women friends to join them.

"Fox holes are democratic. Are You?" and "I invested five sons in the invasion," read signs they carried during their silent protests. One of their approaches was downright delicious. The white women would order food; when their meals arrived, they would promptly pass them to their colored friends, who would eat them while the rest of the customers looked irritated or puzzled. Some whites weren't aware that colored couldn't eat at the lunch counters. A few news reports stated that some white customers even wrote or telephoned the protesters, encouraging them to keep on fighting. Yet store management insisted that white patrons would not accept integrated eating facilities. Although the demonstrators were peaceful and quiet, the managers threatened the women with arrest for trespassing. Two of the Negro women who owned property complained that their banks had threatened to call in their mortgages if they didn't stop their activities.

After conferring with one attorney who urged them to stop the sit-ins because they could be arrested, they went to see my father. Daddy advised them that in Missouri trespassing on a public place could only be enforced if there were some kind of damage done. It didn't have to be physical damage; in fact, profanity and swearing would count. He told them that the best thing for their cause would be if they were arrested because it would hit the newspapers. "I told them that I didn't believe any of these stores would be stupid enough to call the police wagon and lock up fine women like yourselves and risk the economic damage," he said. "So I told them, you keep on going, go ahead down there. I'll represent you."

The CCRC continued its sit-ins without reprisal (or results) until Saturday, July 8, when forty Negro women and fifteen white women sat in at all three major department stores. This time, the stores closed their lunch counters. The mayor's Race Relations Commission offered to act as a broker for the women if they would stop their actions, and the CCRC complied. The commission grappled with the "problem" into 1945 without much movement. Largely composed of whites, it had no real authority and was slow to take a stance on desegregating the stores. One of the stores, Scruggs-Vandervoort-Barney, which Negroes didn't patronize much, known as it was to cater primarily to the "carriage trade" (rich whites), was the first to act. It opened its downstairs lunch counter to all. Another, Famous-Barr, offered to build a separate (but equal) lunch counter, which the CCRC refused to accept. The CCRC did not endorse Scruggs's action either because the store still refused to serve Negroes in its upstairs dining room. Some considered the CCRC's discontinuation of the sit-ins a mistake because it had abandoned its most effective political tool. The mayor's commission only took note of the group's actions after the July 8 sit-in, as did the *St. Louis Post-Dispatch*. It would take a decade before downtown eating establishments at drugstores, five-and-dimes, and department stores began to "open up" through the efforts of the Congress of Racial Equality (CORE). "And that's the way she goes."

In the midst of CCRC's struggle, my father's name was put forth to become the new NAACP president of the local branch. He didn't campaign for it but was elected in November 1944 to a two-year term. It brought him rewards but also tons of criticism. By the next election in 1946, some members were calling for his defeat, saying he was incompetent, derelict in his duties, and out for his own economic gain. He won anyway. He had his defenders, too, one of whom was Howard Woods, who wrote for the *Chicago Defender* newspaper as its St. Louis correspondent. In part, he countered the attacks by saying, "We have heard him accused of 'dereliction of duty' while in the thankless job as NAACP president. We've heard him branded as a 'no-gooder'; . . . Yet, when trouble arises, when police are on the prowl with bloody night sticks and smoking .38s, it's always Dave Grant you find on the scene snooping that big arrogant head of his into what worries belligerent coppers most." Furthermore, Woods said, "We've seen him clear his book of a lot of his regular lucrative practice, while he hied off on another volunteer case."

He chose not to seek a third term in late 1948 but remained a lifetime member of the organization, and he served as part of its institutional memory of the branch through the 1950s. Before his presidency, Daddy penned the "Credo of the American Negro Citizen"[1] for the NAACP branch in 1942. Besides the local NAACP branch, the national Black Elks and other large Negro groups adopted it as their statement of belief. My mother had it framed and tacked it up on a wall in our home. When my father died four months after the birth of his first granddaughter, Mother made me promise that I would make sure that she, and any siblings to come, read it for a glimpse of their grandfather's vision.

As NAACP head, he fought many local monsters. He carried a diminutive casket before the school board headquarters to protest the killing of a ten-year-old student at the Wheatley School. He and others blamed overcrowded classrooms. (After his tenure, he organized a benefit to expose these conditions, with Josephine Baker as its main attraction.) In the fall of 1945, *Carmen Jones,*

---

[1] See addendum.

the Negro version of Georges Bizet's opera *Carmen,* opened at the American Theatre. Le Vern Hutcherson, who was well known to St. Louisans by having performed at the Municipal Opera, had the male lead in the show. Negroes, however, could only hear his magnificent voice[2] from far above the stage in the last balcony. This triggered an all-out assault on the theater's seating policy. "They put us up there in the peanut gallery or the peanut roost, whatever they called it," my mother complained. Mass picketing began, led by the NAACP. "I carried a banner around the American Theatre because some colored people would go down there to see plays," Mother added. As time went on and the weather turned sour, enthusiasm dwindled except for Henry Winfield Wheeler, who never missed a performance; that is, he never missed picketing one, matinee after matinee, and night after night, oftentimes the lone picket in the rain, sleet, and snow. Two years before the American closed its doors for renovation, it opened them to all patrons on an equal basis.

Daddy sought to have W. C. Handy, the composer of the "St. Louis Blues," officially recognized at the Jefferson National Expansion Memorial, already being planned for in the 1940s. In my father's letter to the chairman of the Memorial Association, he said, "No city in the world has been the beneficiary of publicity comparable to that received by St. Louis through the world-famous 'St. Louis Blues'. . . . Its lilting, plaintive phrases await our unborn generations to the end of time." Little happened.

The NAACP took on smaller problems, one of which threw my father into a very public contest with an esteemed, senior member of his own family. Negroes were finally beginning to

---

[2] Le Vern Hutcherson dubbed Harry Belafonte's voice in the Hollywood film production of *Carmen Jones.*

replace whites who delivered milk, door-to-door, in colored neighborhoods. Members had been instructed to keep tabs on any of their neighbors who balked at the new arrangement, out of a self-loathing they weren't even aware of. Some Negroes didn't want their own making deliveries to their homes, feeling it was "better" to have whites wait on them. It would take decades before the Black Power movement of the 1960s exposed this psychological drama. At one gathering, my father asked for a report. A member of the audience had to be prodded by those around him to speak out. As Daddy told it, the man didn't want to mention names but would only give the block where one customer was stubbornly refusing to receive her milk from black hands. "Now, we've got to expose these people. Tell me the name," he insisted. "Well, Mr. Grant, it's your grandmother," he answered. The audience roared, with my father being the first to laugh and shake his head. "Thank you. I'll pay her a visit."

His paternal grandmother, Mrs. Almeda Thomas Riddle Grant, was a former slave who had migrated from Kentucky following emancipation. The only photo I ever saw of her, which sadly vanished from our collection, showed a stern-looking woman dressed in a black, tightly buttoned-up suit coat and almost drowning in an enormous feathered collar. My father adored her, but my mother was less smitten. She recounted that when she met Mrs. Grant, the first thing the older woman said to her was, "Let me take a look at you," and then added, "Are you a schoolteacher?" When my mother answered to the contrary, Mrs. Grant looked askance and said nothing more.

Daddy was clear when he went to see her: "Grandma, I hear you don't want Negroes bringing you milk," he said. "That's right, Davey!" she interrupted him with a laugh and a slap on her knee. He then tried to persuade her to cooperate and emphasized his leadership position in the movement. "And I can't have my family publicly against me," he told her. I don't remember whether she relented or not. She was in her nineties by then and died shortly thereafter; Daddy didn't press her too hard, but it made for another great "and that's the way she goes" story.

Later in the decade, Thurgood Marshall and my father did battle once again in the assault on restrictive covenants—a lawsuit that originated in St. Louis. Unfortunately, this time they fought each other. Daddy didn't tell me all of the details because he genuinely admired the future Supreme Court justice; but after this duel, their friendship changed drastically. When the Supreme Court decided to hear *Shelley v. Kraemer,* the case that would end racial discrimination in housing, in 1948, the NAACP's legal office in New York, which had put housing as one of its top priorities, assumed a lawyer other than George L. Vaughn would try the case. They felt that Vaughn, who had shepherded the case through a series of appeals for over three years, "lacked the sophistication and skill necessary to properly handle the intricate complexities of restrictive covenant litigation and that he was not sufficiently versed in the newer style of sociological arguments."[3] My father, as head of the NAACP branch, and Mr. James T. Bush Sr., a prominent Negro real estate broker who, in large part, had financed the case, refused to bend to the national office's will. Mr. Bush and my father exchanged fiery letters with Thurgood Marshall: They both stood squarely behind George L. Vaughn, Daddy's father's Bass Clef Club singing buddy. Thurgood Marshall wanted to work "with" Vaughn, but the St. Louis attorney instead tried the case along with Herman Willer, a Jewish

---

[3] Jamie R. Graham, with research by Girl Friends, Inc., St. Louis chapter, *Shelley vs. Kraemer: A Celebration* (St. Louis: The Chapter, 1988), 31.

lawyer whom he had met at a conference on restrictive covenants. They won the case, and Vaughn became immediately famous. He received a federal judgeship but died in August 1949 before assuming his post.

Shortly after Daddy was fired from the Circuit Attorney's Office, he became intimately attached to what he described as "the Negro march that was so successful it didn't take place!"; that is, the National March on Washington (MOW) movement, which arose when the first March on Washington, planned for July 1941, did not take place. He joined Theodore D. McNeal, international field organizer for the Brotherhood of Sleeping Car Porters, and organized the St. Louis MOW unit. His participation in this movement would weave itself through almost everything he did for the next four years.

More than twenty years later, when 250,000 people walked down Pennsylvania Avenue to the Lincoln Memorial in 1963, I knew it was not the first time such a march had been planned.

7.

THE FIRST MARCH ON WASHINGTON

So Successful That It Didn't Happen

*T*HE FIRST MARCH ON WASHINGTON (MOW) IN 1941 WAS the brainchild of A. Philip Randolph,[1] a leader of exceptional intellect and foresight who founded the Brotherhood of Sleeping Car Porters (BSCP). The call for this event forecast "an all-out thundering march on Washington, ending in a monster and huge demonstration at Lincoln's Monument" to "shake up white America. It will shake up official Washington." Scheduled for July 1, 1941, it drew attention to the inequities in opportunities for Negroes in all phases of the national defense program, including the armed services, as the nation geared up for its entry into World War II. Government contracts were creating millions of new jobs, but Negroes, if hired at all, were largely relegated to the lowest-paying, unskilled sector of the market. The navy and army were still segregated, and Negroes were completely barred from service in the Marine Corps. The Army Air Corps had reluctantly just begun an "experiment" by allowing Negroes to train as pilots in Tuskegee, Alabama.

---

[1] A. Philip Randolph was instrumental in the 1963 March on Washington.

'BURY JIM CROW' Three of the speakers. They are, from left: Milton P. Webster of Chicago, a member of the National Fair Employment Practices Committee; A. Philip Randolph, founder of the March on Washington movement and president of the Brotherhood of Sleeping Car Porters, and Walter White, executive secretary of the National Association for the Advancement of Colored Peoples.
—By a Post-Dispatch Staff Photographer.

Milton P. Webster, A. Philip Randolph, and Walter White at the MOW rally at the Municipal Auditorium. St. Louis Post-Dispatch. *August 15, 1942, p. 4C. Reprinted with permission of the* St. Louis Post-Dispatch, *copyright 1942.*

The idea for a march took root in early 1941 when A. Philip Randolph "had dreamed up this idea of ten thousand Negroes going down Pennsylvania Avenue," according to Theodore "Ted" D. McNeal, who would become Missouri's first black state senator in 1960. A Pullman porter himself in the 1920s, Ted had taken the lead in getting porters to stand alongside Randolph. The Pullman Company was firing its "Georges" right and left for even listening to "union" talk. Ted held some of the initial meetings in St. Louis after hours, with shades drawn at a shop that was in a black neighborhood and was owned by a Jewish tailor who was sympathetic. Ted's duties included traveling throughout the United States to arrange meetings where Randolph and others would speak about the union's activities. Randolph and Milton P. Webster, the brotherhood's first vice president, now wanted him to stay behind in order to stir up interest in the march and persuade Negroes to come to Washington, D.C.

President Franklin Roosevelt ignored the imminent demonstration for a while but eventually invited some Negro leaders, excluding Randolph, to the White House. They told him that Randolph wanted an executive order directing "war" plants receiving government contracts to hire Negroes; Roosevelt countered by saying he would do nothing with a gun (i.e., the march) to his head. Shortly thereafter, he dispatched the Federal Bureau of Investigation and U.S. Army Intelligence to investigate (two Negro officers did nothing but follow Ted). "They reported that Randolph was wrong when he said 10,000. They estimated that there would be 50,000 Negroes there," Ted recounted. Some predicted that as many as 100,000 blacks would be marching down Pennsylvania Avenue.

President Roosevelt eventually responded with a lukewarm memorandum directing the Office of Personnel Management to include the entire "productive power" of the United States in government work. Considering the memo insipid and meaningless, the MOW went forward with its plans for the July 1 march, but on June 25, Roosevelt issued Executive Order No. 8802. It began: "Reaffirming policy of full participation in the defense program by all persons, regardless of race, creed, color, or national origin, and directing certain action in furtherance of said policy."

The order quashed the March on Washington but gave birth to a national movement, conceived to keep tabs on its implementation. March on Washington Committees, or "units," formed throughout the United States, with St. Louis's and those in Chicago; Washington, D.C.; New York; and Los Angeles evolving into the most influential.

My father became involved immediately. He and Ted were close friends and they organized the city's MOW committee shortly after Randolph came to St. Louis in early May 1942 to address a group of fifteen men and women, especially handpicked for their commitment to civil rights. Besides outlining MOW's philosophy and nonviolent, direct-action techniques, Randolph focused everyone's attention on the pressing need for such an organization in the St. Louis area. Defense industries were thriving in the city and offering plentiful employment, except to colored, who were effectively barred. Advertisements in white dailies candidly called for white applicants to join in "the home front fight of production." No attempts had been made to draw on the vast pool of unemployed Negro labor in spite of an acute need for workers. In fact, these industries even scrubbed off the out-of-work whites from the extreme southeastern tip of Missouri (known as the Bootheel) and imported them to St. Louis to take jobs. When St. Louis Negroes were hired, they were given token employment—as porters and common laborers—with no opportunity to advance to the skilled or semiskilled ranks. Randolph was also adamant that the MOW membership be restricted to the black community, feeling that Negroes should solve their own problems. Randolph would be labeled by New York attorney general Mitchell Palmer as "the most dangerous Negro in America."

Ted chaired the MOW unit, and my father became his de facto vice chair. Daddy always talked about what a lethal team he and Ted were in those days. He explained how they tweaked the "good cop, bad cop" strategy with white authorities, converting it into more of a "hothead, level-head" duet. "My friend's a bit 'touched,'" one of them would say after the other stomped out of a negotiation. "I am much more reasonable; I think you and I can work something out, right?" They became so adept at the game that they usually decided who would do what just before they opened the door to the meetings. "I'm tired of being the good guy; it's your turn, Dave," Ted might say. "Seeing those guys look terrified when one of us started hollering was priceless," Daddy told me.

The unit first met on May 16 in the BSCP office at the Peoples Finance Building. An adjoining room would later be rented as MOW headquarters. "That building had a lot of activity going on there during those days," Daddy remembered. "We set the membership fee as low as we could so almost anybody could join. I believe it was 10 cents a year." About thirty Negroes, men and women between the ages of eighteen and sixty-five, attended. They represented various community organizations, such as the National Association for the Advancement of Colored People (NAACP), the Elks, and trade unions. The membership remained fairly constant, but the unit garnered little enthusiasm from the Negro community until word spread of what was happening at the United States Cartridge Company, commonly known as the Small Arms Plant. On the same day as the first meeting of the MOW, management there began dismissing Negro porters. The company had reluctantly hired them as a way to satisfy the requirements of President Roosevelt's executive order and to muffle Negro demands for war industry employment. This event inspired the St. Louis MOW unit to act. Ted McNeal fired off a telegram to Washington to complain, and with Daddy, who quickly was named "field captain," scheduled a protest against the plant for June 20. The timing of Randolph's visit could not have been better; he laid the groundwork for the unit to grapple immediately with the incident in progress.

The first MOW demonstration was effective and peaceful, as they all would be. At least 250 people marched, ranging in age from their late teens to late sixties. Nearly every profession was represented: doctors, lawyers, teachers, businessmen, cooks, laborers, even employees of the plant who didn't work the day shift. Once the marchers assembled outside the plant, a company spokesman announced plans to train Negro machine workers and to establish an entire factory unit manned by Negroes. The demonstrators listened respectfully and, undeterred, began their protest. While the demonstrators were not permitted to enter the grounds, the employees and officials working inside could still see the placards they carried:

RACIAL DISCRIMINATION IS SABOTAGE!
TWENTY THOUSAND WORKERS AT SMALL ARMS PLANT IN
PRODUCTION—NOT ONE NEGRO!

The atmosphere surrounding the demonstration was charged: Onlookers, both black and white, drove their cars alongside the protesters; armed police officers revved their motorcycles on the sidelines; squad cars roared past; and news photographers frequently flashed camera bulbs. That day, the temperature topped ninety degrees and the route was four miles long. Not one person defected. They withstood the heat for two hours and then dispersed. Their mass protest immediately produced results: The plant hired about seventy-five Negroes and extended a 10 percent pay hike in hourly wages to black employees with the most seniority. Moreover, the plant enrolled seventy-five Negroes in a

Negro marchers in yesterday's "anti-discrimination" demonstration as they approached the small arms ammunition plant administration building on Goodfellow boulevard.
—By a Post-Dispatch Staff Photographer

Marchers in the Small Arms Plant protest. Theodore McNeal is third from right. June 21, 1942, p. 4A. Reprinted with permission of the
St. Louis Post-Dispatch, *copyright 1942.*

job-training program, and shortly thereafter, the number totaled two hundred.

I'll never forget the first time I saw that plant. I got my first paycheck there as a clerk typist when I was sixteen. By then, it was known as the Bullet Factory and was churning out munitions for the Vietnam War. My father drove me there the first day, pointing out where he and the others had marched. There were lots of people in the hallways who recognized him, with black employees almost everywhere we turned. I was quickly identified as Lawyer Grant's daughter, and I felt scrutinized by all. All of the typists (mostly black), myself included, sat at desks in a huge, hangar-like space while supervisors (mostly white) circulated and eyed us distrustfully. It was the worst job I've ever had. Fortunately, another job opened up in city hall, and I snatched it. Even though I only lasted a week at the Bullet Factory, my father was delighted that his daughter had a job there. The baton was beginning to be passed to me.

Following MOW's success at the Small Arms Plant, the unit steadily grew. Negroes of all stripes joined: "discharged porters, disgruntled former defense work applicants, interested professionals, civic leaders, common laborers, and the general run of the unemployed."[2] Ted and Daddy decided to stage a rally like the ones other units were having. With Randolph's agreement to participate, they chose the ten-thousand-seat Convention Hall of the Municipal Auditorium (soon to be renamed Kiel Auditorium and eventually the Scottrade Center) as the venue for an August 14 rally and paid the $450 rental fee. An all-out publicity campaign began in early July.

The day before the event, a parade, composed of approximately one hundred automobiles with placards advertising the meeting and led by the Cole Elementary School band, made its way through nearly every Negro district of the city. Volunteers made cold calls to residents in Negro neighborhoods and requested that they turn off all their lights from 9:00 to 9:15 on the evening of the event, which they did. The MOW utilized radio spots as well as "trailers" in the Negro motion picture theaters to advertise the gathering.

---

[2] Louise Elizabeth Grant, "The Saint Louis Unit of the March on Washington Movement: A Study in the Sociology of Conflict" (master's thesis, Fisk University, 1944), 54.

Some people lined up outside of the auditorium as early as 4:00 p.m. to get a good seat. The program began around 8:00 p.m. to a less than full house. Ted opened the assembly with a brief address, ending it with these pungent words:

> We are here to dedicate our time, our money and our lives to the cause of the United Nations in the fight against the Axis powers. At the same time, we dedicate our time, our money and our lives to the task of burying American Jim Crow in the same grave with Hitler's Nazism, Mussolini's fascism, and Japanese imperialism.

By 10:00 p.m., the audience had swelled to between nine and ten thousand men, women, adolescents, whites, and out-of-towners, including Negro members of the United Mine Workers in Alton, Illinois. Walter White, NAACP executive director, also came from New York to speak. Officers from the FBI and local cops positioned themselves throughout the audience, and troops from Jefferson Barracks surrounded the outside of the auditorium. Some whites remained until the close of the program and applauded with genuine appreciation; others walked out at various times, even in the midst of the speeches, offended by what they heard.

The rally lasted more than four and one-half hours, with most of the audience remaining until Randolph's last words filled the auditorium at 12:30 a.m. Before adjourning, the organization resolved to send a cablegram to Mohandas K. Gandhi in support of India's struggle for independence. It read:

> The March on Washington Movement hails the struggle of India for independence. We pledge you our moral support for freedom and the victory of the United Nations Negro people of America who are also fighting for their democratic

rights. Winning democracy for India and the Negro is winning the war for democracy.

The local newspapers covered the event widely with photographs of the jam-packed auditorium and quotes from the main speakers. The unqualified success of this gathering, coupled with the unit's ensuing actions, propelled St. Louis's MOW into the forefront of civil rights activism for the next three years.

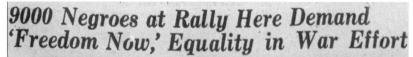

DAVID M. GRANT   A. PHILIP RANDOLPH   WALTER WHITE

Three of the speakers at the Municipal Auditorium rally: David M. Grant, A. Philip Randolph, and Walter White. August 15, 1942, p. 3A. Reprinted with permission of the St. Louis Post-Dispatch, copyright 1942.

The crowd almost filled the Municipal Auditorium for the civil rights rally.
August 15, 1942, p. 1c. Reprinted with permission of the
St. Louis Post-Dispatch, *copyright 1942.*

The members began a string of protests—some successful, others not. The first ended up in the latter category. It was waged against the Carter Carburetor Corporation because of its all-white workforce and its stance to remain so, despite the government contracts it held. On August 29, between three hundred and four hundred people gathered at Tandy Park, a recreational field used exclusively by Negroes. They walked a scorching, St. Louis–summer mile to the company's headquarters, opposite the old Sportsman's Park baseball field, home to the Cardinals and the Browns. The marchers began their protest in front of the plant and were dwarfed by the stadium on the other side of the street, as if sandwiched between not one, but two adversaries. The Cards were a much-celebrated team, but they also represented one of the most bigoted in baseball. Sportman's Park was still segregated, and the Cards would not integrate their team until the mid-1950s, one of the last teams to do so. The Cards were playing that day, and many of the white spectators in the top tier of the ballpark gawked at the procession below rather than watch their ball team whip the Philadelphia Phillies. "Carter employs 3,000 people . . . not one Negro: Is that democracy?" read Ted McNeal's placard. Jordan Chambers's sign demanded, "Shut our mouths and stop our marches with jobs, democracy and freedom." My father's read, "President Roosevelt Says, 'No Discrimination!' St. Louis War Industries Reply 'Says You.'"

They took on the Board of Education, insisting that it design technical training for Negroes commensurate with that provided to white students. They protested against a proposal to redraw city ward boundaries, accusing the sponsors of gerrymandering to make it more difficult for black voters to elect their own to the Board of Aldermen. They joined with the NAACP and the Negro Businessmen's League and agitated successfully for passage of an equal rights bill in the state legislature that would make it a misdemeanor to deny any citizen equal rights in restaurants, hotels, taverns, theaters, or public conveyances. They won. Decades would pass in Missouri before a public accommodations act was enforced but at least something was on the books. They backed a drive, led by my father in 1943 and described in the previous chapter, for the equalization of teachers' salaries throughout the state. The unit vigorously involved itself in the downtown department store sit-ins, also discussed earlier.

Theodore McNeal, Jordan Chambers, and David M. Grant protest against Carter Carburetor Corporation, August 29, 1942. Reprinted with permission of the St. Louis Post-Dispatch, copyright *January 19, 1992.*

They used a novel letter-writing technique by sending a sixty-by-forty-inch postcard to President Roosevelt at a cost of $3.41. Thirty-two local black organizations signed on to its message, which protested the cancellation of a federal hearing of their grievances scheduled in St. Louis.

Beginning in March 1943 and running through the following October, the MOW fought a duel with the public utilities corporations. In discussions with these companies, management used various excuses as to why it couldn't hire more Negroes: They lacked proper skills; the community was not ready to accept blacks in certain positions of responsibility; many higher-level jobs were already filled; and plant management was in favor of integrating the floors if only the unions weren't fighting its efforts.

Southwestern Bell Telephone received the brunt of the unit's attention since its policies were the most blatantly biased. Negroes purchased roughly 10 percent of the telephone company's services, yet they held about 1 percent of the jobs, and all of them as porters. The unit printed and sold penny stickers to Negro telephone subscribers so they could paste them to their phone payment envelopes. The "stamps" read: "Discrimination in employment is undemo-cratic. I protest. Hire Negroes now." They marched against the company, three hundred strong on June 12, and staged an en masse telephone bill payment—in pennies—by two hundred MOW members on September 18. The phone company did nothing until threatened with a permanent picket, scheduled to begin on October 25. Southwestern Bell then unveiled plans to open a branch office in a Negro neighborhood that would be operated by blacks. It quickly added that the customers would be under no obligation to pay their bills there, not wanting to appear as if they were establishing a Jim Crow office.

In 1943, MOW went head-to-head once again with the infamous United States Cartridge Company. Negro workers turned to the MOW and outlined what had been brewing at the factory for months, such as the company's refusal to upgrade competent Negroes into supervisory positions and the placement of less qualified whites over skilled Negroes. They also described the embarrassment they felt when white women employees chose to strike rather than supervise them. Ted and Daddy began negotiating with management, but nothing worked. On June 3, all Negro personnel, approximately 3,600 black men and women, went on strike when a white foreman was promoted into a job that black workers believed should have been filled by one of them. The MOW encouraged them to return to their jobs, feeling the strike would undermine their efforts. All workers did, and the MOW's subsequent negotiations resulted in more Negro employment, opportunities for upward mobility, and higher-paying jobs in general. Colored workers began replacing white foremen at an accelerated rate; in fact, on one day alone thirty-two Negroes received appointments as foremen. Ultimately, U.S. Cartridge would employ six thousand colored people.

Throughout the 1940s, both Ted and my father were under surveillance by the FBI and by Army Intelligence, as was the MOW unit and the NAACP, in general. Daddy used to talk about the moles. They were all military men, dressed as civilians. He remembered one colored fellow who actually divulged his identity to them. He told the leadership that he would still be black after the war was over and that he believed in what they were doing. He promised he wouldn't make up any lies about the organization's activities in his reports, and he would even identify other informants as they were sent to survey the organization. My father got so used to having a "snitch" in the audience that he said he was able to spot one as soon as he walked in. Ted's recollection was even sharper. He learned about one, assigned from Army Intelligence headquarters in Omaha, through the director of the YMCA where the soldier was living. "Finally, about three months later, I blew my stack, pointed him out to the membership one night and, of course, they yanked him right away and sent in another fellow." It was his replacement who confessed his undercover role to the MOW and pointed out the next guy who came in. Furthermore, Ted recalled "threats on the telephone late at night . . . someone would call me a lot of obscene names and say they were going to blow the house up and this sort of thing but that was the extent of the threats."

If my father had been harassed, he never mentioned it to us. He never saw his FBI file but said he knew that "there was one up in Washington." If he had, he would have called it "a whole lotta nothing and just plain wrong." I later filed a Freedom of Information Act request, and what I saw was fairly boring reading. It contained inaccuracies about some of his employment and innuendos about his association with the Communist Party in Missouri. My mother had attended one of the party meetings with him and was startled when he didn't interject. "Dave just sat there and didn't say a word. It was so unlike him; I guess he knew not go on the record there," she remembered. My father wasn't Communist hostile until he realized that they were "phonies," trying to infiltrate the NAACP for their own purposes. They had opposed MOW's picket of the Small Arms Plant, circulating leaflets calling the action a mistake. He'd conferred with the head of the party in Missouri, and the file states that the NAACP had used the Communist Party's office equipment. Although he always said that they pestered him to join, he never did and became less and less willing to associate himself with them as time went on. It seemed curious to read that he was voted in as vice president of the Book Shop Association, a known Communist front, but that "Grant had never been seen at the Book Shop since he was elected to that office."

What I could not evaluate were all of the paragraphs and sentences removed from the file. At least part of each page, sometimes

90 percent of what was written, had been censured and remains "classified" to this day for reasons known only to the FBI. The thirty or so pages covered my father's activities and whereabouts (Chicago; East St. Louis; Washington, D.C.; New York City) from 1942 to the early 1950s, concentrating on his MOW and NAACP work. He was described in a June 1943 report as a "negro, who has been the militant leader of the March on Washington Committee in St. Louis, Missouri, and who was instrumental in stirring up the negro population there to seek jobs in industrial plants after the President's Executive Order, 8802, was issued." One thing the FBI rightfully acknowledged was that my father was "a speaker of renown."

As World War II came to a close, Ted and Daddy would remain in the civil rights fray but would add another organization to their portfolio. The MOW felt its techniques were becoming outmoded. They wanted to add their battles to the ones being fought in the courts, and the NAACP could do that for them. They felt that Ted should continue leading the MOW; Ted suggested that my father take the reins of the NAACP, having already served as its counsel. My father was proposed for president of the local branch for the term beginning in late 1944. "I had not been attending meetings, and I told them that I would accept it if elected, but I wouldn't campaign for it," he admitted. He won the position with the full weight of the MOW behind him, and most likely a number of the women members who had sat in at the downtown department stores.

As the MOW's activities ended, Ted returned full-time to his BSCP duties, but he did not limit himself there. Few people know of his role in the Montgomery, Alabama, bus boycott, so famously sparked in 1955 by Rosa Parks's refusal to give up her bus seat to a white man. Mr. E. D. Nixon, who led the Montgomery branch of the BSCP and also served as president of the local chapter of the NAACP, called Ted shortly after Mrs. Parks was arrested, saying that they needed money to organize a boycott. Ted went to the local Teamsters Union chief and managed to collect $10,000, which was the first money to arrive in Montgomery.

In spite of the constant tug-of-war between the St. Louis unit and local corporations, it is estimated that by the time St. Louis's MOW unit disbanded, Negroes had secured between fifteen thousand and sixteen thousand new jobs because of its efforts. Besides these tangible gains, the organization served to build and sustain the morale of the black community in general through its weekly meetings, special mass gatherings, and representation at similar assemblies in other cities. Negroes knew that the MOW was a venue where their grievances would be taken seriously and weighed fairly. At its height, the MOW boasted an active membership of over twelve thousand. Although some of the jobs were eliminated shortly after the war ended, Ted McNeal underscored the fact that "blacks, for the first time in large numbers, gained skills that could get them other jobs."

8.

What a Fabulous Party!

Entertainment in Jim Crow's Shadow

*M*UCH OF NEGRO ST. LOUIS WAS AWARE OF THE WORK of the National Association for the Advancement of Colored People, March on Washington, and other civic organizations and participated, directly or indirectly, in their activities. But, as the saying goes, "There's a time and a place for everything." Black St. Louis was also known, even in the late 1800s, for its tradition of parties and get-togethers in peoples' homes, private clubs, and the few public venues available to them. Jim Crow didn't allow for many "places," so they found one or created one because there had to be time put aside for some fun. As everyone from my parents' circle has told me ad infinitum, "We couldn't go anywhere or do anything. Everything was restricted, so you had to do it yourself."

One word seems to sum up the "talked-about-for-months parties" that St. Louis Negroes put on during Jim Crow days: "FABULOUS." Any discussion started there and skyrocketed. Whether the event took place in the penthouse ballroom at the Peoples Finance Building, the Municipal/Kiel Auditorium, the

Elks's private club, or in someone's home, everyone was breathless by the time the last word was spoken. The party pinnacle was the formal dance where "everyone would be dressed to the nines," my mother gushed, with the women in long gloves and gowns (some of them daringly backless) and the men in tuxedos. "Everybody would get so excited just thinking about going to one. They were very well attended, and the boys were all on their best behavior. They didn't have Afros, that's for sure," she assured me.

The earliest such occasion recounted to me took place on New Year's Eve 1931. The Royal Vagabonds, a men's club, was founded in the first part of the twentieth century by some of society's leading citizens, that is, schoolteachers, postal employees, businessmen, and such. The "Vags" soon became known for their lavish bashes, and in 1931 threw a New Year's Eve dance in the Peoples Finance Building's penthouse that is remembered to this day. The members were distinguished by wearing white turbans embedded with gold insignia and ribbons that swung to and fro. At the foot of the staircase leading from the fourth floor to the ballroom, three Vags welcomed each of the four hundred guests who attended that night. At the top, two pages in blue outfits and floor-length capes checked the names of each invitee and bowed. The hall itself was barely lit to simulate dusk, so much so that those approaching from outside thought that there may have been some mistake. "Why aren't the lights on? Did they cancel the party?" Once inside they were awestruck by the décor. "Merry Christmas" banners dangled overhead and multicolored bunting draped the walls. Iridescent lights danced across the floor, up the walls, and onto the ceiling overhead and reflected off a huge, mirrored sphere suspended above the dance floor. Alternately showering green, then rosy red light on the revelers below,

Mildred Hughes Grant, ca. 1930.

the effect was so baffling that it took a while to figure out. People finally realized the source: two roving lights placed on the stage next to the bandstand and pointed at the hanging ball. Above the stage, purple and yellow bulbs (the club's colors) flickered, announcing, "Welcome! Royal Vagabonds."

Those who weren't dancing congregated near a booth, labeled "Aquae" and "Drink." The "waters," however, were not given freely; they required a password (which was changed every twenty minutes) and had to be whispered to the bartenders. Off to one side, an oversized, artificial flower bud sat, almost unnoticed. Just before midnight, the Royal Vagabond Presentation March began with the members and their partners leading the line. Suddenly, all of the lights faded and a spotlight fell on the forgotten flower. "It must have been midnight when I jumped out of that big flower and did my pirouettes back and forth across the hall, dressed like the New Year Baby," recalls June Gordon Dugas. She was the six-year-old daughter of one of the Vags's founders and she announced the New Year "with trumpet held high," according to the newspaper account. "They put me behind the curtains off to the side of the stage and told me to nap until my turn came. I did anything but that," June said. At every opportunity, she peeked outside and took in the swirling colors, fancy clothes, and nonstop motion. Above all, she remembers two distinct sounds. "There was so much laughing and a lot of whispering," she told me. The march then began in earnest with streamers snaking through the room, threaded over the necks and arms of all, and ultimately tying up their feet as they partied on. "It was a dance," wrote one of the journalists the following week, "this dance of the Royal Vagabonds, that made everybody forget that home had not been so lively these holidays and made more than one say that here is one social group which had shown 'vim, verve and vitality,' and what does one say? More power to them!"[1]

I don't know how long that party lasted, but the guests, most likely, headed straight to their houses afterward to recuperate for the next day's festivities. New Year's Day itself had to be celebrated at home or at a friend's by eating an abundant meal, the centerpiece of which was a tureen filled with black-eyed peas, believed to bring money one's way during the next twelve months. Those who could afford it added a goose to their menu.

After some formals, the guests headed off to the Elks Club, a Negro men's charitable, fraternal society with its headquarters in a spacious brownstone. Officially titled the Improved Benevolent Protective Order of Elks of the World (the IBPOEW), it was founded by B. F. Howard and former slave Arthur J. Riggs in 1898 when the Caucasian precursor refused entry to colored men.

"They'd rent it out, you know," my mother told me. "It was one of those elegant houses out on Enright Avenue with high ceilings, beautiful woodwork, and parquet floors. It was THE place to go after a dance was over. It was a private club, and you'd go there to keep on talking and partying. It was a small space and wasn't built for dancing because it was a house and the Elks office, but they had a staff to serve drinks and hors d'oeuvres," she said. At some point, the organization moved, and a doctor and his wife bought the house. They continued these after-parties on the first floor of their minimansion. "Everybody was trying to make money, so Dr. and Mrs. Vaughn opened their house for this. We couldn't go to the fancy restaurants or hotels," my mother added to the chorus.

---

[1] Copy of a newspaper article, no date, no name. Probably from *The St. Louis American* or *The St. Louis Argus*, early January 1932.

It was not unheard of for a gentleman to add a finishing touch the day after by sending a gift to his date. He might have had a pair of lovebirds delivered to her home with the words "They mate for life" pinned to the cage, as one of my mother's suitors, an elevator operator, once did. "He came from a good family but he just wasn't interested in education after high school. He worked in one of those buildings out on Lindell," Mother explained.

More informal affairs took place in one of the halls at the Municipal/Kiel Auditorium, sponsored by a social club or one of the fraternities or sororities, even though the Greeks loved throwing formal events. When they were allowed to, Negroes could "book" certain nights at the auditorium or on the SS *Admiral,* an excursion boat docked on the levee. The women or juvenile girls (since age groups intermingled freely) wore short cocktail dresses, and the men and boys, suits and ties. People opened their homes for formals, cocktail or dinner parties, and "club" meetings (bridge, sewing, charitable work, and book clubs). Whatever the occasion, everyone dressed accordingly. My mother used to say, "Everybody was trying to outdress each other!"

One of the men's clubs stood out. It began, casually at first, in the early 1890s with a group of men who would gather to celebrate each other's birthday. Formalized in 1892 as the Gentlemen's Birthday Club, a year later it incorporated under the name Anniversary Club and exists to this day. Although its genesis was social, it soon took on a serious tone when the men stated that "important topics of the times" had to be discussed. When possible, nationally known figures, such as Booker T. Washington, president of Tuskegee Institute in Alabama, would address the members and their guests. Other rules were simple but strict: All events were formal, that is, tuxes and long gowns; all whose birthdays fell in the month of the meeting were designated as the "hosts"; and a toastmaster had to be in charge. The founders and earliest members of the Anniversary Club included educators, doctors, and a relative of mine, James W. Grant, who ran his own dancing academy and was considered black St. Louis's "authority on public decorum."[2]

June Gordon Dugas remembers that one of the parties in the 1930s at her parents' mansion on Enright Avenue included an analysis of a Sinclair Lewis classic. "Lewis had won the Nobel Prize, and everyone was talking about *Main Street, Main Street, Main Street,*" she noted. "The parties were quite mixed at our house . . . all ages and backgrounds. My father was an educator, so there were always lots of them but there were postal workers and municipal civil servants. My mother played piano beautifully so she, and anybody else who could, would entertain the guests on the grand piano we had. Everyone wore long gowns and tuxes or dark suits, and my brother and I got to watch what we could from the upstairs landing."

In the late 1870s, June's grandfather, David E. Gordon, and other Negro educators from the East Coast had been recruited to move to St. Louis to become principals in the colored schools. A group of St. Louisans, led by Billy Roberson, a barber and member of the Negro Chamber of Commerce, met one evening in 1877 and took it upon themselves to find Negro role models for their children. Until then, only whites taught black students since St. Louis had few trained colored teachers so soon after the Civil War. The highly educated blacks who came to St. Louis would fill all of the positions in Negro schools over the next few years. Eventually, whoever became principal was even able to rename his school as he wished. Until then, colored schools were only identi-

---

[2] N. B. Young, *Your St. Louis and Mine* (St. Louis: Author, 1937), 60.

fied by numbers. My maternal grandmother entered a numbered grade school on her first day but finished at Benjamin Banneker, in honor of the eighteenth-century black astronomer. The Phyllis Wheatley School had been called simply Colored School No. 7 long before my father matriculated there. But as soon as he started, Daddy and all of his classmates knew the story of the Negro nineteenth-century poet from Boston. David E. Gordon took over as principal of the L'Ouverture School, named after the liberator of Haiti, Toussaint L'Ouverture.

Benjamin Banneker Grade School graduating class, 1893. Eliza (née Elizabeth) Holliday at age fourteen, third row from bottom in the middle. Photo from Your St. Louis and Mine *by N. B. Young, 1937. Courtesy of Saint Louis University.*

This group of educators became leaders in the civic, fraternal, and social development of a city that had sought them out, and St. Louisans revered them for it. David E. Gordon and several others from this group founded the Anniversary Club. Frank J. Roberson, who may or may not have been related to Billy Roberson and would eventually design our house in south St. Louis, also came from the East Coast to teach art. Gordon's son, Curtis Inge Gordon, was one of the Royal Vagabonds founders. These elders brought a heightened sense of black culture to the community. Arthur Freeman, my father's beloved principal at Wheatley, was referred to as "the one and only J. Arthur Freeman"[3] for his leadership and decorum, along with his "beautiful lyric tenor voice," as Daddy described it.

Another instance of a formal house party took place after my parents eloped in 1944. Grandma was disappointed, having hoped for a church wedding at All Saints, but my grandfather was delighted. Daddy loved to recite Grandpa's concise reaction. "Son, you just saved me a lot of money." At least it gave Sarah, my mother's godmother, a reason to spend some. She immediately went downtown and bought yards of silk fabric, then opened her sewing machine and began stitching a new formal gown for herself. At the same time, she mentally sketched out a menu for the celebration she would throw at her home on Enright Avenue, a few blocks from the Vaughns'. Sarah's husband, Dr. Josephus Gregg, was one of a hundred and a handful of black physicians at the time. They both loved to show off their home. Silk taffeta covered the walls, Persian rugs (two of which I still own) almost totally smothered the sparkling wooden floors, most of the furni-

---

[3] Ibid, 12.

ture was upholstered in brocade, and a paisley pattern in bas-relief swirled up the radiators. With a $500 down payment in hand, the Greggs had moved from east of Grand Avenue to Enright Avenue in the late 1920s. By then, Josephus's practice was exploding in spite of the well-known fact that he treated many of his poorer patients for free. One of the first black couples to move onto Enright Avenue as whites fled farther west, they also arrived just in time to have their new home damaged by the tornado of 1927. They quickly recovered and turned their house into a showcase.

Mildred and David Grant at the reception at the Gregg home to celebrate their marriage, 1944. Sarah Gregg is in the background.

Mother said that Sarah probably did the grocery shopping for the party herself at the Union Market. She went there almost daily because Josephus only trusted her hands to pick the freshest fixings for his dinner. She had a small army of helpers in the kitchen and a lead cook who may have prepared some of the food elsewhere and brought it to the party.

When I used to visit the Greggs as a child, the house was wondrous to me. I remember that Sarah had the biggest vanity mirror I'd ever seen—it went from floor to ceiling and wall to wall in her dressing room. I always wondered if the house had been built around it. They even had an imitation color television set that they crafted by stretching a tricolored, transparent covering across the screen to simulate the earth at the bottom (green), sky at the top (blue), and the part in between (some shade of yellow, I think).

House parties weren't all as orchestrated as my parents' wedding reception. Some were thrown together so friends could just talk and eat together. On occasion, they also offered the unexpected. A celebrity in town to perform might drop by a run-of-the-mill gathering, brought there by the local impresario or a friend. In fact, that's how my mother met Cab Calloway, who eventually became my godfather. "It was just an ordinary party, and in walked Cab. He was so handsome and famous at the time. It must have been sometime in the 1930s when I was home from college," my mother said. Over the years, she and Cab developed a friendship and she even introduced him to one of her dearest girlfriends from Chicago, who became his second wife and my godmother. Although his appearance that night was unplanned, it was not so unusual. The black community made sure that performers and nationally known figures had someplace to go to unwind and mingle with the locals.

The best clubs during those days, both opened in the 1930s, were the Club Plantation and the Riviera. The Jeter-Pillars Orchestra was the Club Plantation's house band from 1934 to 1945 and THE big band to have for formal events when they were available. James Jeter and Hayes Pillars, both saxophonists and originally from Arkansas, directed up to fifteen musicians and were known for their musical prowess and professionalism. During the summers the club shut its doors because of the heat but Jeter-Pillars traveled to outdoor venues in Kansas City to play.

Mr. and Mrs. Cab Calloway in a 1949 Christmas photo.

The Jeter-Pillars Club Plantation Orchestra. Courtesy of the Jeter family.

The Riviera consisted of a room with tables and chairs, a long bar, and a stage. Jordan Chambers made sure all of the Negro big bands and most of the famous black performers in the United States played at his club, along with the Jeter-Pillars Orchestra, when he could snatch them away from the Club Plantation for an occasional gig. He also made certain that St. Louis's summer temperatures didn't keep paying customers away. He had blocks of ice (hundreds of pounds' worth) delivered to the attic and installed industrial-sized fans that swirled refreshing, "washed air" throughout the club. It was damp air and may have put a crimp in the women's hairdos but was soothing nonetheless.

"Dave never liked to see a woman sitting at a bar alone or with a girlfriend but he said that was the only place [the Riviera] where you could go with a girlfriend and have a drink. Chambers had big bouncers there because nothing was going to happen that would give the police a reason to come in there," my mother explained to me. The Riviera wasn't just a nightclub; it was the center of his political machine where he held strategy sessions. Chambers's inner circle, the black and white movers and shakers of Democratic politics, could always enter the "back bar," with those less well connected relegated to the "front bar," which was open to all. It was in the back bar that Chambers and others (my father included) hatched a moneymaking (for some who got in on the ground floor) pyramid scheme that ran wildly through the north side in the late 1940s. My parents even used the language of the "'game" to announce my birth.

Gail Milissa Grant's birth announcement, using the pyramid game as a model.

Political tactics were not on the agenda of another well-known men's club, started in the early forties. The Lamb's Club, whose theme song's lyrics were "We're poor little lambs who've gone astray, Baa, Baa, Baa," only had fun on its program. They threw parties but the men gathered mostly to play cards and joke with one another.

By the late 1950s and early 1960s, some house parties may have become less formal but they still had lots of sparkle. There were so many parties that the women joked that all they did was just sit around, waiting for the next party, until they got involved in desegregation efforts and their focus changed.

But in the meantime, they let their imaginations take over. One of the girls' clubs transformed the Vagabond ballroom into a Japanese teahouse. They made a red *Koshi* shrine and surrounded it with cushions and low tables decorated with cherry blossoms. Invitations were mailed inside of long tubes; they had to be unfurled in order to read the details, written in Japanese-like script. The members wore Asian garb, with one member topping her costume with a copy of Maria Callas's headgear in *Turandot*. Another time, the women's Art Club instructed everyone to come as their favorite painting.

There was another class of entertainment in St. Louis that the Negro community anticipated with delight all year long: the Y Circus and the Annie Malone Parade. My parents didn't reminisce about these events, but their friends who lived on the north side did. The circus lasted three or four nights, took place every spring at Kiel Auditorium, and was sponsored by the Pine Street YMCA, which used it as a way to fund the Y's Camp Rivercliff in Bourbon, Missouri. The kids would show off their gymnastic skills, for instance, as part of the show, and all of their families would come along with others in the community. The greatest draw would be the professional bands and singers. Stars like Count Basie, Duke Ellington, Sarah Vaughn, Nat "King" Cole, and Billy Eckstine all played the Y Circus. Lesser-known acts, such as Joe Jiggy Johnson, Lucky Billender, and Dusty Fletcher, a comedian, came as well. Attorney Ira Young, Judge N. B. Young's son, remembers his affiliation with the Pine Street Y with nostalgia and affection. Attending summer camp for him was "one of the most rewarding experiences that I've ever had. We learned so much about basic things, about nature, about camping out, about living together, getting along together, communicating."

Then on the heels of the Y Circus, the Annie Malone Parade took center stage each spring. Ms. Malone became a millionaire when she created a treatment that claimed to make black hair grow long and shiny. She started out in Lovejoy, Illinois, in 1900 and moved to St. Louis shortly thereafter. By 1918, she installed her business, named Poro Beauty College, in the heart of St. Louis's Ville neighborhood. She donated the grounds for the orphanage, and the annual parade soon became a staple for the neighborhood. There is no way I could approach the depiction that Attorney Forriss Elliott, who attended them all growing up, wrote for me:

> All the scouts, fraternal organization, Greeks, geeks, wannabes; you name it. Every organization in town was there to march and show out. The old men of the Elks with their hats of elk horns and badges of merit ribbons hanging off ribbons on their chests. The Masons, the Eastern Stars, the no-name groups,—"just in the parade, honey." Then the church sisters, the "Women's Auxiliary" of this church or that, the "nurses"—the ladies that gave you smelling salts and fanned you when the Spirit overwhelmed you—all these ladies dressed in starched whites made a wave of virtue as they resolutely kept time with the drummers' cadence. The bands

were from the schools, the fraternal organizations, and the police department. Everybody tried to out-play, out-dress, and definitely out-step the other group. A few seemed a little tipsy from either the heat or from a swig off the communal alcoholic "taste." This just livened it all up and made it all the mo' better. When somebody you knew passed by, you'd yell to them and they'd do that little extra skip or cha-cha-cha-step to let you know they heard you. I have never seen a parade like those—we did parades! And yes, the white and black politicians were in them, riding in convertibles with Miss Harlem Tap Room in a bathing suit on the fender, and other beauty queens slinking alongside the cars handing out campaign literature or balloons or favors. I almost forgot the funeral homes. They'd drive the hearses and flower cars, and have people passing out their fans.

Poro College, 4300 St. Ferdinand Street. Photograph by Dorrill Studio, 1942. Missouri History Museum.

Some of black St. Louis's most important educational, cultural, and social institutions stood within a two-block radius of the orphanage: Sumner High School, Homer G. Phillips Hospital, Stowe Teachers College, Tandy Park and Community Center, Poro Beauty College (which housed the Lincoln Law School), Antioch Baptist Church, St. James African Methodist Episcopal Church, Billy Burke's Restaurant, and the Amethyst Theatre.

But then there was the "Hub."

9.

THE HUB

The Peoples Finance Building

*O*NCE CITY HALL BOOTED MY FATHER FROM THE CIRCUIT Attorney's Office in 1942 for his part in the Sikeston lynching protests, he reestablished a private practice in a one-room office in the Mill Creek Valley area. He soon needed more space, so by early 1943 he moved into the Peoples Finance Building at 11 North Jefferson Avenue where he'd already spent numerous days and nights working with the March on Washington (MOW) movement and the National Association for the Advancement of Colored People (NAACP). He rented a three-room corner office on the third floor with a southeastern exposure and an expansive view of downtown. My mother would eventually work in the central reception area between Daddy's office and another for a lawyer who would share the suite. Margaret Bush Wilson had just finished Lincoln Law School, and my father hired her immediately. She worked as his secretary, legal assistant, and, on occasion and much to her surprise, substitute in court. One Monday morning, Margaret dashed off to court when my father hadn't arrived in time to make it to a divorce proceeding. "I'd been shadowing him all along but I'd never tried a case. To this day, I will never know whether he deliberately didn't show, so I would either sink or swim, or if he really was 'recovering' from a too, too exuberant weekend!" she reminisces whenever we laugh together about her training. She left his office after her apprenticeship to work as a U.S. government attorney (which Daddy never understood), and broke new ground when she was elected the first woman president of the local chapter of the NAACP in the 1950s and, ultimately, the first woman of color to chair its national board of directors.

According to the late Benny Rodgers of the *St. Louis American,* the Peoples Finance Building was the handiwork of two brothers, the Inges, who were medical doctors. They raised the funds and built the first Negro-owned commercial property of its kind in St. Louis. It housed the first black-owned bank in St. Louis, started by Dr. B. J. McGraw, who taught economics at one of the schools. Unfortunately, it dissolved during the crush of bank closings in the early 1930s. Elementary school students at the time were especially upset when that happened. Their teachers had initiated a savings program where the students would contribute a penny at a time to their individual accounts. Once they had accumulated a dollar, the teachers put it into the bank for them. The late federal judge Theodore McMillian, a family friend, was in grade school at the time and told me that he had a dollar in the bank. When the bank went bust, he went looking for McGraw: "You know all about economics. How come you couldn't save that bank?" he wanted to know.

Furthermore, the Inge brothers couldn't hold on to their enterprise during the Depression, and it fell into the hands of Jewish investors. Yet it carried such cachet that many black St. Louisans still remark, "Anybody who was anybody had his office in the Peoples Finance Building." The lineup of tenants included most of the St. Louis branches of black national organizations. Among them were the Brotherhood of Sleeping Car Porters; the NAACP; the Colored Motion Picture Operators; the Missouri Pacific, Wabash, and Frisco Dining Car Employees; and the March on Washington unit. In addition, the building housed *The Saint Louis American* newspaper; the J. Roy Terry School of Music; Jos. T. Bush and Co., Realtors; and Harold Young, photographer, who by now had eclipsed W. C. Maxwell as St. Louis's premier black photographer. Chicago's Supreme Liberty Life Insurance Company had its branch there as well.

Peoples Finance Building, Jefferson Avenue and Market Street. Photograph by Dorrill Studio, 1935. Irv Shankman/Allied Photocolor Collection. Missouri History Museum.

Professionals—doctors, lawyers, and dentists—also had their practices there. By the 1940s, the Peoples Finance Building became known as "the Hub" of black political activity in St. Louis. The proximity of leaders in the community and membership institutions fighting for change developed into a brain trust where an almost daily cross-fertilization of ideas was unavoidable. These exchanges were assisted by the Deluxe Restaurant, situated directly across Jefferson Avenue and owned by impresario Jesse Johnson. It was one of the few restaurants where Negroes could sit down for a meal and be served in St. Louis, and the Finance Building's tenants usually streamed across the street for lunch. Professionals, civil servants, and blue-collar folk alike came there from downtown and across Jefferson Avenue, turning it into the Negro equivalent of a golf course's nineteenth hole where deals were brokered and talk was valuable. If you wanted to know what was going on, you went there and listened. The tables were big, and people just sat down wherever there was a free chair to join in on conversations always worth their time. People also patronized two smaller restaurants along the Jefferson Avenue corridor. They were both owned by the Ford brothers, Al and Lafayette, and called the Turf Grill No. 2 and the Ford Brothers French Fried Shrimp Shop. The latter, which served only shrimp, gleaned its recipe from a similar eatery in Chicago run by a cousin of the Fords.

The Peoples Finance Building was crowned by a dazzling penthouse ballroom, and no invitation to one of its events ever went begging. Apparently, the stock market crash couldn't dim its lights immediately; in December 1929, Alpha Kappa Alpha, the first Greek-letter Negro campus sorority, held its annual gala, the Boule, on the top floor. And no one could forget June Gordon Dugas's prancing across the dance floor as the Royal Vagabonds rang in 1932. Jesse Johnson booked every big-name musician that he could find to play in the penthouse. Some women, barely teenagers at the time, remember having their first dance with their fathers in that ballroom.

The shops were wonderful, too. Mr. Harris, a Negro pharmacist, ran the drugstore with a soda fountain that had the best Coca-Cola. Dave Margulies, a Jewish man, started the Peoples Liquor Store there and would replicate his gold mine throughout St. Louis, transforming it into the leading chain for spirits until his company was gobbled up by a corporation. In its heyday, the Peoples Finance Building hummed with activity and purred like a well-fed cat.

By the time my parents wed in September 1944, Daddy had a growing business. His secretary took another job shortly after their marriage, so my mother said she'd help him until he could find a replacement. Located just around the corner from where they first lived with her parents, they could stroll there leisurely in less than five minutes. She pinch-hit for him for almost ten years. As soon as she arrived, she straightened up the office. Once my mother had the walls repainted and the floors refurbished, it was clean and orderly, albeit sparsely furnished.

"Dave was very patient and careful to show me how he wanted to present different papers. I learned a lot because I didn't know anything about the legal system or being a legal secretary," she explained. He trained her how to prepare wills, divorce pleadings, probate petitions, and everything having to do with real estate. I remember interrupting her when she mentioned property since I didn't recall my father talking much about having a notable real estate practice. "You took anything that came through the front door," Mother answered me with a laugh.

She then gave me an example of a typical real estate client in those days. A gentleman in his forties would appear at the front door of the office, sit down in front of her, and say, "I found a house that I want to buy and I think I need a lawyer." He'd then pull out four or five thousand dollars in cash and lay the stack on her desk. On cue, she'd take pencil and pad in hand and begin asking questions. A Pullman car porter by trade, he had been working for more than twenty years and had finally saved up enough money to purchase a home outright for himself and his family. By the time my mother finished taking notes and putting him at ease, she'd have a new client for her husband. Furthermore, this nameless man represented one of the many working-class folk who came to my father's office during the 1940s seeking legal counsel—workers from the Scullin Steel Mill, waiters, street cleaners, railroad men, preachers, chauffeurs, seamstresses, and elderly ladies who had managed to buy buildings with rooms or apartments to rent. Daddy had little tolerance for the details of the civil side of his practice, preferring to concentrate on criminal law, especially anything that smacked of racial discrimination.

He always managed to be out of the office whenever one of those landladies had an appointment. They habitually would show up with bags full of every receipt they had ever received from their tenants and a long list of items they just had to discuss with *their* lawyer, Attorney Grant. My mother handled them with aplomb and, as a result, she developed friendly relationships with the clients. She respected them, and they recognized and appreciated her concern. Her work was so accurate and comprehensive that at times my father never laid eyes on the clients with civil claims until he met them outside of the courtroom. He spent an enormous amount of time at the Law Library, remarking that any lawyer who shunned research wasn't much of an attorney. Mother could always tell a little old lady, "I'm so sorry, but my husband is deep in the stacks of the library, working for you right now. But I'd be glad to go over everything you have in that sack with you."

She went on to remind me that all Negro attorneys were in general practice in those days. "You couldn't afford to specialize in one area. So many black people were going to the white lawyers back then. They felt that if they showed up with a Negro representing them, well, they felt they wouldn't win," she admitted. Worse yet, according to one newspaper editorial, appearing "in court with a Negro lawyer was like signing your own death warrant."[1] My father, however, did cordon off two types of offenders—pedophiles and drug pushers—emphasizing his distaste for them. "I know I couldn't give them my best defense, representing them," he often told me. My father's instincts were sharp, and he usually knew whether his client was guilty or not, even if they insisted otherwise. I wanted to know how he could defend accused murderers, especially when he knew they were far from innocent. "Everyone deserves the best possible defense in court because that's the law!" he would answer without elaborating. I knew to press him no further. My mother also said that "Dave didn't like to fool much with prostitutes and pimps either."

But everything else was fair game. It had to be, given that the odds favored white lawyers in those days. Morris Shenker, a prominent Jewish attorney, "had a tremendous black clientele and he was great on civil rights," my mother remembered. "He tried to get your father to go into his law firm but Dave didn't want to. You see, a high percentage of Shenker's business came from black clients, and then with Dave's public persona, well, Shenker could have had even more. Your father could have made a lot of

---

[1] Editorial, *St. Louis American*, September 18, 1975.

money with Morris but he didn't want to be known as a pawn." My father's unrealized dream was to start his own black law firm. He scouted out properties (and took me to see one with him) but never managed to get the capital to do so or convince enough local lawyers to take a chance with him.

In retaliation, Daddy would practically forbid us from patronizing Caucasians for any professional services: no white doctors, accountants, dentists, etc., allowed. He even once admonished me when, in the late 1970s, I brought home a jar of jam bottled in Anniston, Alabama. "Do you know what happened there on Mother's Day in 1961?" He then told me how civil rights workers had been firebombed while riding on an integrated bus. "We can never forget these things or where they took place." he emphasized.

Negro attorneys had to get up earlier and stay up later than anybody else—literally. Judge Billy Jones of East St. Louis credited my father with helping him establish his practice by doing just that. In the mid-1940s when Judge Jones returned to the area after law school and "was unable to make expenses," he came to my father's office for advice. Daddy had already offered Jones a place in his office when they met at Jones's graduation from Howard University's Law School. Jones, however, wanted to establish himself in his hometown. He complained that some ministers and political leaders were steering blacks to big, white law firms and that he couldn't get cases. "When do you arrive at your office?" Daddy queried, "and when do you go home?" Dissatisfied with Jones's answer, he told him to come in earlier and stay open later. He told him to find or make opportunities to speak before groups. He counseled him to go to Sunday school at one church, the 11:00 a.m. service at another, and the afternoon gathering somewhere else—not just occasionally but each and every week. He advised him to get active with the lodges and described the activities of the NAACP. But above all, he admonished, "Get a cause and stick with it! And East St. Louis is *pregnant* with causes."

Some members of the Mound City Bar, 1937. Bottom five: Harvey V. Tucker, Robert L. Witherspoon, Virgil Lucas, Joseph L. McLemore, Edwin F. Kenswil. Top eight: Silas E. Garner, DeWitt Lawson, George Wade, William H. Parker, N. B. Young, Ellis Outlaw, Harrison Hollie, Ambrose A. Page. From N. B. Young, Your St. Louis and Mine *(St. Louis: Author, 1937). Courtesy of Saint Louis University.*

Jones followed his advice, amassed clients, and became the attorney for the East St. Louis NAACP. On January 31, 1949, his cause made the national news. He and others led Negro children into nine all-white, half-empty schools and began a school sit-in to protest busing and Jim Crow education in East St. Louis. By noon, the school board closed the schools and called an emergency session. On the third day of protest, at my father's urging, Judge Jones announced he would withdraw the children from the white schools and pursue the matter in the courts. "Dave kept telling me that some child may get hurt or killed and that the people would then blame me and turn against me. He said, 'Billy, you have made your point. What further good is to be gained in continuing to try to get in their schools? The thing to do now,' he said, 'is to go to court.'" Judge Jones, with my father as co-counsel, filed the case, lost at the circuit level, and appealed the ruling. After two years of litigation, with my father guiding him "in the research, the preparation, and the presentation of all the legal matters, incident to the lawsuit," Judge Jones said, East St. Louis schools opened up to all children, followed by theaters, restaurants, and drive-in movies.

My mother also filled out tax forms, simple as they were in those days, for which they charged their clients $3 or $4. There was very little so-called corporate work, as black businesses had just begun to incorporate. The unions also needed legal counsel and divided their dealings amongst a slice of the fifty or so Negro attorneys then practicing law.

Daddy's passion was on the criminal side, and it showed. Some eventually declared him to be the best defense trial attorney in the city (without inserting the usual qualifier of "Negro" between "best" and "defense"). One of my father's protégés told me that, as a teenager, he overheard a man, barely into his twenties, say that he was about to go after someone because he had saved enough money to get Morris Shenker or Dave Grant to defend him so he wasn't worried about going to jail! Daddy zealously took on those accused of armed burglary, murder, assault, assault and battery, aggravated assault, assault with intent, and so on. "There was a *lot* of assault in those days and a lot of it associated with alcohol," my mother remembered. Daddy, however, relished representing a client who claimed that a policeman had assaulted *him,* since the underlying cause usually led to some sort of police brutality or harassment based on race. My father would remain a trial attorney for his entire career. Whenever there was talk of a judgeship coming his way, he made it clear that he wasn't interested in changing sides. "I didn't want to have to send people to jail, decide how long they'd have to stay there." I know he also didn't want to have to alter his life outside of court, turning his back on some of his "questionable" buddies in town. My brother and I wondered if his regard for this rough-and-tumble aspect of the law was so strong because of his own hotheadedness and his visceral understanding of where rage could lead a man. He sympathized with many of his criminal clients and always took their backgrounds into account.

As already mentioned, throughout the 1940s the Peoples Finance Building was the scene of scores of gatherings, official and informal, where civil rights strategies were discussed and implemented. The colored lawyers who participated in these sessions nurtured each other daily, sharing information that could assist them in their jobs. They'd talk about the peculiarities of the judge they'd just stood before or the prosecuting attorney's personality or the intricacies of a legal brief they'd just submitted. They'd take attorneys who were new to town to meet court officials. Frankie Freeman, the first woman appointed to the U.S. Commission on Civil Rights, remembers my father doing just that once she decided to open her own law practice in the late 1940s. "I hired a secretary-receptionist and had some business cards printed, then Dave Grant took me downtown and introduced me to the judges in the civil and criminal courts. I told them I was willing to be appointed to pro bono cases that would give me important exposure."[2] Before she knew it, that day or the next, one of the judges gave her the first criminal case of her career. Daddy also introduced her to Jordan Chambers and told her to get active with the Democratic Party and the NAACP.

Ted McNeal always brought national news from the Brotherhood of Sleeping Car Porters Union; he may have just been on the phone with A. Philip Randolph. N. B. Young (an attorney and future judge) and Nathaniel Sweets, struggling publishers of the *St. Louis American* newspaper, could be counted on to divulge "news" before it was printed or obtain grist for an editorial. They all commiserated over their losses, which may have been more numerous than their victories, but those who still remember being privy to these meetings "took heart in listening to these fearless men battle the injustices of the world."[3]

They lent moral support, as well as any loose change they could spare, to members of the Moving Picture Operators' Union (an American Federation of Labor affiliate) when they conducted an unauthorized strike in the mid-1940s. The black community had six movie theaters. The members wanted the whites who worked at two of the "black" theaters transferred to white theaters, rather than importing white operators into the city to service exclusively

---

[2] Frankie Muse Freeman, *A Song of Faith and Hope: The Life of Frankie Muse Freeman* (St. Louis: Missouri Historical Society Press, 2003), 43.

[3] Editorial, *St. Louis American,* September 18, 1975.

white theaters, as was the case. Their unemployed union brothers, they reasoned, should have those jobs. Going to the movies was an especially sore spot for black St. Louisans. The first-run films took weeks to get into the black theaters, and some never made it. A friend of my parents moved to San Francisco in the 1940s and she told me that she couldn't wait to go to the movies. She went to three in one day just because she could. She didn't remember or even care what she saw.

When a black attorney won a case or settled a score, it was a collective triumph. One story will always stick in my memory. I listened to it countless times from my father and was fortunate to have heard one unforgettable recounting by the late Benny Rodgers. In the late 1940s, Daddy was at the Clayton courthouse defending a man accused of murder. On the first day, the judge recessed the trial at noon and gave everyone an hour for lunch. Daddy got in his car, drove to the Deluxe Restaurant, had lunch, and returned to court just before 2 o'clock. "The judge was on the bench," he emphasized. In all of my dad's stories, he only had to say those words and I understood the allusion. It meant that the judge was mad as hell and that you had better have a life-or-death reason as to why "Hizzoner" had to wait for counsel. When questioned by the judge as to why he was late, my father explained calmly, "Well, Your Honor, there is no restaurant anywhere near your courthouse that will serve a Negro, so I had to drive into town to get some food, and I just got back. I lost my parking space nearby the court so I had to walk quite a ways here." Caught completely off guard and visibly annoyed because he couldn't chastise my father, the judge could only say, "Let us proceed."

The next morning when the trial began, the judge told Daddy that he had called the Cheshire Inn, just down the road, and instructed the management to serve him at lunchtime. At one of the breaks, my father called Benny and invited him to lunch at the restaurant. Benny, with skin the color of gingerbread, loved to tell this part. He said that my father wanted to make sure that there was no mistaking him for anything other than a colored man so he took Benny with him. They sat down and ate. As they finished their meal, my father said, "There's just one more thing I have to do before we leave." He walked to the men's room while the whole place stopped talking and watched him, and stayed there for a long time. When he returned to the table, he told Benny that white folks really hate it when we use their restroom "facilities," except he used another word for it. He then wiped his mouth ceremoniously with his napkin, stood up, and slapped a $5 tip on the table. Daddy went back to court, and Benny returned straightaway to the Peoples Finance Building and spread this public accommodations "victory for all" throughout the halls faster than the roadrunner could have. He may have embellished his telling of it, but everybody expected that.

The attorneys collaborated on lawsuits, drawing on each other's expertise; a prime example was the case against Washington University in St. Louis. Daddy, Robert Witherspoon, and George L. Vaughn filed suit against the university in 1945. The school refused to admit American Negroes but accepted students from the Caribbean islands, the Indian subcontinent, and Africa. The attorneys' tack was aimed at the school's pocketbook through its tax-exempt status on real estate holdings in St. Louis. In short, they queried, "How could a private institution go public on one day of the year—tax collection day—and remain private on the remaining three hundred sixty-four?" which was exactly what the university had been getting away with for decades. By 1945, Washington University was saving nearly $500 a day by not paying taxes on $6 million worth of off-campus property. "Let them PAY for racist policy," my father said. They lost the suit on the first go-round, and it lay idle for seven years while they prepared to take it all the way to the Supreme Court, if necessary. It ruffled enough feathers during this time that the university began to integrate, department by department, until 1952 when the whole school opened up. Attorney Vaughn's son was the first Negro admitted to the Law School. I had no idea that my father's involvement with this would have repercussions for me. He wanted one of his children to graduate from the school he "went after," and Washington University became my alma mater.

When national figures such as Ralph Bunche, the first American Negro to win the Nobel Peace Prize for his part in ending the 1948 Arab-Israeli War; Roy Wilkins, who followed Walter White as NAACP executive director; Adam Clayton Powell Jr., one of the first powerful African American members of Congress; or the inimitable Thurgood Marshall came to St. Louis, they usually made a stop at the Peoples Finance Building. They were famous, to be sure, but also approachable and part of St. Louis's extended family. Some of them stayed in the homes of their friends since decent hotel accommodations were often off limits to them. According to Benny Rodgers, Mrs. Mary McCleod Bethune, another early civil rights activist and founder of a college for Negro girls during the early twentieth century, and W. C. Handy, world-famous composer of the "St. Louis Blues," both refused to stay at one of the few hotels that catered to Negroes, the Booker Washington Hotel, because it was white owned. They preferred a Negro-owned rooming house.

I only remember the Peoples Finance Building after its prime. My father usually took me there after one of our "dates." He would take off an occasional afternoon and come home to pick me up before I started kindergarten, so the two of us could spend time together. By then, my mother had left my father's practice to stay at home with my brother and me. So she and the housekeeper would dress me up, and I would wait for him to arrive. We'd go to the zoo or the Jewel Box, an indoor botanical garden in Forest Park, before returning to his office for what remained of the day.

Even without firsthand knowledge of the hubbub that once filled its halls and offices, I still thought it was as exciting place. For me, it was more like a giant dollhouse with grown-ups to visit and adult-sized furniture to arrange. Daddy's office was simple and seemed filled perennially with sunshine. By then, many of the offices were empty and some hallways were dim. I had the run of the place and no one ever came looking for me. I was free to skip through the spacious corridors as I wished, open doors without knocking, and be greeted by my parents' friends with smiles and hugs, and sometimes a sweet treat. I climbed the marble stairs or rode the elevators, with their brass accents, at will, escorted by the operator on duty. He made sure my fingers didn't get pinched in the accordion-like door. The drugstore had a soda fountain and served hamburgers and malted milk shakes and sodas. The owners spoiled me silly, and I loved spending time roaming through the rows of shelving and drinking root beer floats with them. I remember walking next to a disabled man who worked in the building. Strapped to a wheeled board on the floor, he would push himself along with his gloved hands. As long as I stayed inside, I felt as safe as if I were in my own home. The neighborhood around the building had further deteriorated since the 1940s when my parents lived with my grandparents. We could only visit them by car, though it was only around the corner, when we left Daddy's office—no walking allowed.

The Peoples Finance Building was swept away in 1960 by the Mill Creek Valley demolition. My father had moved his office to another St. Louis landmark—the Wainwright Building designed by Louis H. Sullivan, famous for its architecture but not for its tenants. The Hub was gone, never to be duplicated.

10.

Hi-De-Ho

Famous Faces from Faraway Places

BY THE TIME MY FATHER SWITCHED OFFICES, MY FAMILY had been living in south St. Louis for about a dozen years. Many well-known figures from out of town who visited the Hub passed by our house as well. My parents' wide array of guests spiced up our usually staid neighborhood whenever they visited us. Friends, some famous, would never have seen the south side had it not been for us, and the residents would never have laid eyes on them. Jim Crow, unwittingly, spawned a sort of "overground" railroad in the first half of the twentieth century and further galvanized local black communities to join the civil rights movement by establishing personal links between them and recognized leaders and show business celebrities. They couldn't stay in hotels, so they stayed at people's homes.

St. Louis's train station, the immense Union Station, facilitated these contacts because almost anyone who went cross-country, and didn't take the northern route through Chicago, had to pass through it. Once the largest and busiest rail terminal in the United States, some claimed in the world, it welcomed or bade adieu to more than 100,000 passengers from every corner of the country on a daily basis in its heyday during the 1940s. Even in the 1950s, the station was still awash in activity and excitement. I loved going there on family jaunts. We watched passengers galloping down the loading platforms to catch their trains, eavesdropped on sweethearts saying goodbye or reuniting, inhaled the gusts of steam that the engines belched, and winced when the whistles hooted. Almost as exciting as a circus, the station's characters and costumes were ever changing. The train shed, covering over ten acres and holding nineteen miles of track, was more overwhelming than a big top. My brother and I also learned how to "eat out" at Union Station; its restaurant, Fred Harvey's, hadn't refused service to colored folk in recent memory. Located on the ground level and partially encased in glass windows, the restaurant allowed us to eat leisurely without missing the spectacle that surrounded us. We carried a certain affection for this restaurant chain because of its color-blind reputation. There were other people, however, who had less-warmhearted memories. It had discriminated earlier, but that was all but erased from my memory until Judge Theodore McMillian told me "his" story. In the 1930s when he was in college, he and a friend, who looked white, ordered a couple of beers there. "We can serve you," said the waiter, pointing to McMillian's "invisible" buddy, "but not him." The judge's friend promptly responded, "Well then, give me two beers." ("Invisible Negroes," as my father labeled them, looked white but never tried to "pass" for anything other than what they were.)

Among the innumerable VIPs that the Union Station welcomed, the unrivaled Josephine Baker stood out when she returned to her birthplace for the first time in years in 1952. Sidney Williams of the Urban League; Howard Woods, now of the *St. Louis Argus* newspaper; and my father, with the *Argus's* backing, had convinced her to headline a benefit concert to raise awareness of overcrowding in the black public schools. They booked Kiel Auditorium's largest space, the same one the March on Washington (MOW) used for its first rally in 1942. The few days Baker spent in her hometown became another staple in my father's collection of stories. It always began, "How in the hell am I going to keep Josephine Baker from throwing a fit and refusing to perform tomorrow night when she learns that the only hotel she can stay at in St. Louis is a dump?" The first time I heard my father begin this tale, I was maybe seven or eight years old and I was shocked . . . shocked because it was probably the first time I ever heard him swear. That curse word got my full attention because I knew he must have really been in a jam. He then said, "I was waiting for Josephine Baker at the train station in Granite City [Illinois] so I could accompany her on the last leg of her trip to St. Louis. And honest to God, I was talking out loud to myself."

It was February 1952 and Howard Woods and my father had traveled to Chicago in December and convinced "La Bakair," as she was known in Europe, to return to her birthplace and perform as the benefit's star attraction. It would be her first professional engagement in St. Louis. Daddy was fairly sure that if he could persuade her to appear, any of the leading hotels would welcome her. But only the manager of a transient hotel, well known for its "short-term" reservations, accepted the booking. A disaster was clearly in the making. No star, no show, no money to pay the auditorium but plenty of egg on my father's face.

Of one thing, however, he was certain. Without first-class accommodations, the show would not go on with Josephine Baker. On this tour, she had already canceled several engagements in cities when the finest hotels would not accommodate her. Several months earlier, she had refused St. Louis's Chase Hotel's offer of

$12,000 per week to sing in its lounge when management mistakenly assumed she would stay elsewhere during her performance.

The Chase's blatant racism had scandalized St. Louis's black community. My father and his colleagues knew Josephine Baker expected them to compensate this time around by securing her a suite at one of downtown's upscale hotels. So there sat my father, reduced to talking to himself in the freezing darkness by the side of the railroad tracks. What could he say to her and to those who had already purchased tickets for the next night's concert at the cavernous Kiel Auditorium? My father had been optimistic when he signed the entertainer before securing an appropriate place for her to stay. He had even gotten Mayor Joseph Darst to proclaim the day of her performance Josephine Baker Day, with a parade and reception scheduled before the event.

As her train approached, Daddy had no idea what to do or say. But an idea came to him almost as soon as he stepped on board. He easily tracked down Josephine Baker and her entourage—hustle and bustle followed her everywhere. Amidst the clamor stood the imposing Ms. Baker with Ginette Renaudin, her French wardrobe mistress, three dainty Siamese cats, and the extremely handsome actor James Edwards. Edwards, who was among the first black actors to trounce on Hollywood's stereotype of black males as shiftless illiterates by playing dignified characters, had been added onto the bill but no one was sure he would be arriving with her. And no one had mentioned anything about the cats. Daddy's long shot of an idea made all the more sense now, given the extent and complexity of her crew. "Miss Baker, I would be honored if you and your company would stay at my home. My wife is out of town and my children are with my in-laws. It's a big house, and I'm alone there. It's quiet, and you can prepare for the concert in peace." Without hesitation, she accepted his "gracious" offer and he quickly forgot the speech he had begun composing in his head to calm the Kiel Auditorium crowd. Whether Josephine Baker surmised why our house unexpectedly had become available remains unknown. She never questioned it, and my father never explained.

The train proceeded to St. Louis. With a smile as broad as the arches that spanned the station's massive yards, Josephine Baker alighted from the train and strode down the platform with the cats, her clothing maven managing a portion of her $250,000 worth of costumes, and the attractive actor surrounding her. She had returned to her birthplace, a city that she said represented "fear and humiliation" for her as a child, and St. Louis greeted her with halfhearted applause.

First of all, the leading daily newspapers put announcements of Miss Baker's arrival next to stories on burglaries and deaths. The mixed or muted reviews of her appearance were similarly placed with scant or no mention of the mayoral festivities. Yet a more destructive plot was afoot to undermine her St. Louis debut, and virtually shelved Baker's career in the United States for the next twenty years. Walter Winchell, one of the most famous newspaper columnists at the time, was responsible. Once an ardent admirer, he had become incensed by her public denunciation of him for not defending her when she was refused service at the Stork Club in New York the previous October. He was at the club that evening but denied knowing about the incident. She said otherwise. So he dipped his pen in vitriol and ignited a backlash against "Miss Josephine Faker" or "Miss JosePhoney Baker," as he henceforth labeled the star. He insisted that, among other things, she was pro-Communist, pro-Mussolini, anti-Semitic, and anti–colored people. Seldom in his career had Winchell gone after someone with such vengeance. His scheming worked. By late 1951, theaters and hotels throughout the country began canceling her bookings. A proposed book project with Flo Ziegfeld on her life was called off, and people in Harlem, New York, often fled when Baker sat down next to them in a restaurant.

St. Louis folk were not fully aware of the growing consequences of Winchell's shenanigans. My father and his colleagues unknowingly overplayed their hand by reserving the largest hall in Kiel Auditorium, which seated ten thousand. According to newspaper accounts, only six thousand to eight thousand attended the benefit—most likely the result of so little publicity. Ever the professional, Josephine Baker ignored the empty seats and dazzled the audience. She sang in French, Italian, Spanish, Portuguese, and English and danced provocatively for nearly two hours. Her costumes ran the spectrum from a Christian Dior, fur-trimmed, bejeweled velvet gown to the *jellaba* garb of a Tunisian vendor. At one point, she laughingly gave her age as forty-five, "not counting the summers." Then during her speech, she insisted that the audience rise from their seats while she lambasted racism in America and extolled the virtues of French liberalism for nearly an hour. Her diatribe may have further antagonized the mainstream press. She never mentioned overcrowding in the St. Louis public schools.

According to some of those who saw the show, she was a big hit. They didn't even seem to notice that the house wasn't full because, in their words, "she filled it up." St. Louis had never seen anything like her, and they loved her because she was one of their own. My father was just relieved that the show had, indeed, gone on.

Daddy never had much to say about his houseguest when he told this story, having moved to the third floor for the duration of her stay. But he always mentioned the cats—how they

Josephine Baker with David M. Grant and a newscaster during the benefit at Kiel Auditorium, February 1952. Courtesy of the Moorland-Spingarn Research Center, Howard University, Washington, D.C., Mildred H. Grant Collection.

daintily lined up, each waiting for the other to finish before performing their toilette, and how Baker fussed over and baby-talked to them.

The day after the show, Josephine Baker packed up her razzmatazz and left St. Louis with as much flourish as when she arrived. She went to Mexico City and Las Vegas for engagements, then undertook an extensive Latin American tour and returned to Europe. She would not revisit her native country for almost twenty-five years. And she never performed in St. Louis again.

So whether they arrived by car or train or less often, by plane, we hosted out-of-town guests, another rarity in our neighborhood. The whole block always turned out when a one-of-a-kind character came to town. There was a doctor who owned a hospital in Detroit, lived with his family in a mansion on Boston Avenue, and hailed from Texas, where, as the saying goes, everything is big. He, himself, was king size, and he wore an equally impressive diamond pinkie ring. He loved to visit his mother in Austin, Texas, by driving back and forth, and he stopped with us along the way. He owned a fleet of automobiles fit for a Motown mogul and housed them in a garage that doubled as his own private discothèque. One car was larger and more lavish than the other but none of them prepared us for the capstone of his collection. First, we heard the three air horns that he blew to announce his arrival. And then the man himself rolled up in his made-to-order bus that slept eight. When he sped along the highways of America, a specially mastered sound system belted out the blues inside and outside of the cabin. Muddy Waters's "Got My Mojo Working" was one of his favorites. Anyone who rode in the front passenger seat sat beside a shotgun, fully loaded, which rested in a hand-tooled, leather holder. When the doctor from Detroit arrived in the bus, it took up half our block; his Lincoln Town Car filled up a little less. He sometimes showed up with a liveried driver behind the wheel and a sable lap robe covering his knees.

My godfather caused another kind of stir. In the 1950s, Cab Calloway was still a household name. He was well known to black St. Louisans, having performed for decades in the Mound City. Back in the 1930s, Jesse Johnson booked Cab at the St. Louis Arena. People still remember that hundreds who couldn't get a ticket milled about outside just to hear his "Hi-De-Hos" waft down from the open windows. Our neighbors just wanted to stare at him, except for our postman, Red, known for his flaming orange, porcupine-like locks. An Irish charmer, he insisted on getting autographs for himself, his wife, and each of their sizable brood. Sometimes he'd bring Cab's records to sign. Even Uncle Cab, who at times was abrupt or reserved with his fans, always gave in to whatever Red wanted.

The Hi-De-Ho man with the gargantuan smile and trademark coal-black, silken locks that he rhythmically tossed from side to side while performing was a fairly quiet presence offstage. In the early 1950s, he came to town with a production of *Porgy and Bess* as Sportin' Life, a character that George Gershwin created in the 1930s with Cab in mind. Uncle Cab was so booked at the time that he couldn't accept the part. It was not until the revival of the play, after the demise of the big bands, that he had enough time to take on the devilish role. I will never forget sitting in the front of the theater, legs dangling from my seat, as I watched agog as the stern, somewhat aloof man I called my uncle turn into a viper onstage. He lured Leontyne Price, as Bess, to go north with him by filling her head with promises of fancy clothes and her nose with something that made her obey him. It seemed to me as if hundreds of people sang their lungs out as they twirled across the stage.

Leontyne Price surrounded by St. Louisans and Porgy and Bess *cast members at the Grant house in 1954.*

I'm not sure if my brother and I went straight to our grandparents' after that weekend matinée, but I know we weren't anywhere to be found when our parents gave the cast party after the second show that night. Someone sent a professional photographer to document the evening when Leontyne Price graced our living room, along with Uncle Cab and numerous members of the cast and crew. From all indications, it was a "fabulous" party, fueled in large part by the cases of Griesedieck beer that were on hand. From the photos, the party could have been used as an advertisement for the beer company, with guests holding their cans up high for the camera shoot. I believe Ms. Price remained a respectable length of time, and after her departure everyone relaxed a bit and partied till dawn.

Other VIPs came and went. Juanita Hall, who won a Tony as Bloody Mary in the musical *South Pacific* and who reprised the role in the Hollywood version, arrived one balmy afternoon with her floor-length mink coat slung over one shoulder. Benny Payne,

Singer Bill Daniels and Benny Payne, his arranger and accompanist.

the pianist and masterful arranger for a string of famous musicians including Cab and Billy Daniels of "That Old Black Magic" and "My Yiddishe Mama" fame, would sit at our piano and serenade us with his own heartrending, never-to-be-published compositions. I learned that he and Billy were two of the first Negroes to have their own TV show in 1952. Negroes on television were so rare that every time I saw one, I'd shout out, "Mommy, Daddy, there's colored on TV!" They'd usually come quickly, and we'd all marvel at the novelty of it.

Lena Horne, America's first major female Negro movie star, never came to Arsenal Street, but I made her acquaintance, as an infant, when she visited St. Louis in the summer of 1949. Nobody seems to remember why she was in town—a singing engagement, maybe, or for the promotion of a new film. Her tour of St. Louis included various stops in the black community, among them my brother's nursery school. Everyone was atwitter with, "Lena Horne's coming, Lena Horne's coming," so Mommy dressed me up and took me there. She knew her slightly through Uncle Cab and Aunt Nuffie and figured she could get some photos of us together. I only know that Ms. Horne and I became acquainted from the "5/15," our home movie, so titled because it captured the first five years of my brother's life and the first fifteen months of mine. It shows her wrapping me in her arms and holding me to her cheek long enough for my father to get it on film—her, in a blood red swing coat and loden green hat that dipped over one eye, and me, in yards of pale pink cotton knit and white organza. Afterward, she pulled the nursery school kids around her and sang to them. She then made a red carpet–type exit, smiling and waving on cue, and was whisked away by her manager. She left everyone speechless with her style, class, and glamour.

Lena Horne holding Gail Milissa Grant, 1949.

Train travel also brought another class of visitor to our neigh-borhood who stood out, but our neighbors barely took notice. They came on serious business. Some of them, if not already known as trailblazers, would be chronicled ultimately in Ameri-can history books as early civil rights pioneers. They stopped by our house or went straight to my father's office to collaborate on lawsuits and discuss desegregation tactics. Walter White, Ralph Bunche, A. Philip Randolph, Roy Wilkins, and Adam Clayton Powell Jr. were among them. I barely remember them, if at all. Maybe they came when I was a toddler or not yet born. I just know that whenever my parents recounted any of their visits, they became more animated. In later years, they both lamented the fact that they hadn't kept a guest book to document all of the famous people who passed through our door. My mother's verbal snapshots of them were telling. "Thurgood was very intense and very earthy and dedicated to the cause of civil rights and what he was doing. But then when the business was over, he was ready to party and he could party," she exclaimed. "Adam Clayton Powell? I think he came to give a speech and there was more of a banquet afterward. He really wanted a party thrown for him. That's what he liked."

David M. Grant with Ralph Bunche, Nobel Peace Prize winner, at Grant's office in the Peoples Finance Building, early 1950s.

In the 1940s, my parents told me that they often went to the Union Station not to pick up anyone but to feed their friends. My mother would prepare a meal and carefully select the menu for its shelf life since it might have to last for hours without spoiling. Negroes could not "receive service" on trains until later in the 1950s, so they had to travel with their own food. The Negro Pullman porters couldn't even serve other Negroes. She usually included fried chicken, hard-boiled eggs, a few candy bars, and ice-cold sodas and placed them all in a shoe box or hatbox. Their friends would give Mommy plenty of notice, by telephone or telegram, of their itinerary before boarding the train, so she had time to cook. On long journeys, my mother's would be one in a string of meals, with other friends doing the same thing along the route. Although Fred Harvey's restaurant was available, there was never enough time to leave the train and sit down for a proper lunch or dinner. So Mother would wait on the platform, with her shoe box or hatbox, spend ten to fifteen minutes catching up on the latest news with her buddies, pass off the goodies, and wave them off. I have one faint scene in my head of standing in the station with Mommy holding on to me with one hand and carrying a shoe box in the other while we waited for someone from Chicago to pass through. At the time, I couldn't feel the poignancy of her there, waiting with such a recognizable symbol of Jim Crow—the "shoe box lunch." For me, every trip to Union Station was exhilarating—filled with the promise of new sights and sounds and smells.

II.

MOVING WAAAAAAAY
DOWN SOUTH

$\mathcal{S}$OME ST. LOUISANS HAVE TOLD ME, "I WOULDN'T GO TO south St. Louis on a bullet" or "I've never even BEEN to south St. Louis." The most haunting comment I've read about residential segregation in St. Louis came from native Debra Dickerson, an author and attorney. In 1972, she and her mother refused to get out of a realtor's car when looking at a house for sale in one of the city's still segregated neighborhoods. She wrote:

> My chest still constricts just remembering those white faces as the residents straggled out of doors to see the niggers look at the empty house next door. The realtor begged but we wouldn't budge. Grimly, my mother would only say, "I don't want to be a pioneer" as she pulled the car door from the woman's hand. She'd already survived 18 years sharecropping in Mississippi and 25 as a manual laborer up North. We knew what the law books said, and we knew what the reality was. We confined our search to the black part of town. No, nobody made us. We just were neither stupid enough nor brave enough to put American justice to the test.[1]

---

[1] Debra Dickerson, "Sambo in the Shadows," July 15, 1999, www.salon.com.

I read her quote a few years ago. It confirmed what I felt as a child. What my family did twenty-five years earlier was a huge step. I don't think they were stupid, but they were brave.

Whenever I asked my parents why they bought a house in south St. Louis in 1947, they always replied, "Elmer sold it to us for $4,000." The dialogue never went much beyond that. Elmer was E. Simms Campbell, the groundbreaking, St. Louis–born cartoonist who was the first black American to have permanent columns in national publications, such as *Esquire* (since its inception in 1933) and *Life* magazines. His family owned our house and I learned that after they vacated it, they rented it to other black families in succession. For the most part, these former tenants formed part of the clan of "invisible Negroes," as my father called them. They might have lived where they did because of Frank J. Roberson, who built our home, the house to the east, and several others nearby. Mr. Roberson, part of the group of East Coast educators who came to St. Louis in the late nineteenth century, taught art at Sumner High School but had also studied architecture in Germany in the 1880s.

Around the turn of the twentieth century, he was responsible for a rash of houses, all similar in plan and size, within five or six blocks of one another. He and his family lived in one; the reclusive Mrs. Lewis, our next-door neighbor, lived in another; and the Wilkerson clan inhabited a fourth. If there were any other houses, whites lived in them. When Mr. Wilkerson died in the 1950s, he had a stash of over $300,000 in his home on Humphrey Street. He had opened a barbershop in downtown's Railway Exchange Building shortly after it was built in the teens, had gotten stock market tips from all of his white clientele, and untrusting of any bank, had kept all of his earnings at home. Negro St. Louis talked about his coup for years.

Edgar Wilkerson, barber; David E. Gordon, principal of L'Ouverture Elementary School; and Frank Roberson, art teacher and architect, ca. 1910.

In any event, on one of Elmer's trips from New York, where he resided in an estate in Westchester County, he decided to let go of his St. Louis house completely. After three years of living at my grandparents', it was time for my parents to move into their own place. Elmer offered them affordable terms and, having little extra income, they leapt at the chance. So on the face of it, the answer boiled down to money.

"Your father was so excited about having his own house that we never talked about the neighborhood," my mother always emphasized. Daddy never said this to me but knowing him as I did, I am sure he felt that nobody was going to prevent him from taking advantage of a good "deal" and the opportunity to house his family—and certainly not some white folks! I also feel that my parents believed that they could handle whatever happened. They'd already faced a lot. Daddy had lived in a neighborhood with whites at the turn of the twentieth century. My mother had attended a Caucasian high school in the 1920s. They both had been stalked by Jim Crow for years. So my parents and brother moved into the nine-room, three-story house at 3309 Arsenal Street, and nothing happened. No protests, no insults, no obstacles—at least not in the beginning. The first serious challenge came in 1950 when my brother David turned five and needed to attend kindergarten. Buying a house south of Chouteau Avenue and fending off racial insults were minor stumbling blocks compared to integrating a public school there.

David M. Grant with his son, David W. Grant, 1948.

Elmer Simms Campbell's art studio in New York City, 1949. Left to right: New York City official Jhn. J. O'Toole, cartoonist E. Simms Campbell, David M. Grant, St. Louis mayor Joseph Darst, David W. Grant, and W. C. Handy, composer of the "St. Louis Blues." Courtesy of the Moorland-Spingarn Research Center, Howard University, Washington, D.C., Mildred H. Grant Collection.

My father had already tangled with a neighborhood doctor during an emergency when, shortly after they moved, David fell down the basement steps and hit his head. Daddy was home alone and panicked, realizing that it would take more than half an hour to take him to our family physician on the north side of town. In fact, David's head injury looked worse than it was, but blood was flowing so Daddy bundled him up and rushed out the door. He ran less than a block away to the storefront office of Dr. Nye and bolted up one flight of stairs. The doctor stitched up my brother in silence and then told my father that the only reason he touched his son was because he was bleeding but that he wouldn't put his hands on him again. He concluded by telling my father to take him elsewhere to have the stitches pulled.

Rather than following his immediate impulse and knocking the man senseless, my father relied on the wisdom of an ancient philosopher: "You took an oath when you finished medical school, the Hippocratic oath, which hangs on your wall right here, and you've broken it. You bet I won't bring him back here because you aren't fit to call yourself a doctor. I'm a man. You can take it out on me but how dare you take your racial venom out on a defenseless child?" Every time I passed Dr. Nye's office growing up, a chill ran through me and I almost raced past the scruffy entrance.

And my mother had butted heads with the Italian American owner of the candy store three doors from our house. She took David into the shop, sat him on a stool, and ordered milk shakes. When the man refused to serve them, my mother told me, "I performed that time." She had noticed religious pictures and statues prominently placed in the picture window. "You're supposed to be a Catholic with all of your saints everywhere. A better word is 'hypocrite'!" she shouted as she pointed to the images and slammed the screen door behind her. "I think he sold the store not too long after that," she laughed. "There was so much prejudice down there," she always said. "But it's interesting because Mack, the barber around the corner from us, cut David's hair the whole time. I just took him right in there."

For me, this type of uncertain reaction to us was confusing and frightening. I came to see it as a powerful "unknowing," and much like playing a game I didn't know the rules to. My house was

Mildred Grant with her son, David W. Grant, 1945.

so safe and warm inside; yet outside of it was uncharted. Where could I go? What could I do?

The schooling dilemma presented itself shortly after my brother went to kindergarten at a black public school on the north side. When my mother picked him up one day and found him and his buddies breaking glass bottles against an iron fence for sport, she decided he needed to transfer. Grant Elementary, located only three blocks away and which, ironically, bore our last name, was off limits. I knew nothing about "separate but equal schooling." I just saw that most of the neighborhood kids went there. But I remember overhearing my parents' whispers: "We can't even think about sending them to Grant; they'd be beaten up as soon as they walked in the door." To this day, Grant Elementary, long ago shuttered, remains a phantom to me, having only seen its façade from a safe distance.

Instead, we trekked nine blocks, what seemed to me an interminable distance in those days and farther than almost anyone else in the school, to Pope St. Pius V Catholic Elementary School. In 1947, a year after Archbishop Joseph Ritter arrived in St. Louis to assume his post, he ordered the Catholic parochial school system to desegregate. More than seven hundred white parents threatened court action, declaring that "separate but equal" schooling applied to parochial schools as well. In a pastoral letter, read at all masses throughout his archdiocese, he threatened excommunication to any Roman Catholic who joined in the lawsuit, and the protesting group decided against any further action. Some Jesuits I've met proudly remark that Saint Louis University integrated its student body in 1945, before Ritter came to town. They always fail to mention that Charles Anderson, a Sumner High School teacher and devout Roman Catholic, helped to shame the university's administration to act. He conducted a lengthy, one-man picket every Sunday in front of St. Francis Xavier's, the university's church, until they gave in.

My parents were so impressed by Ritter's bold move that they decided to send us to St. Pius. We were definitely strangers in a strange land at first—the only nonwhites and the only Protestants. My brother rebelled against the rare bigoted nun, received his share of the *N*-word, was pelted with punches from his classmates, and threw some before they could. He was smart and would deliberately defy any nun, less clever than he, with his brainpower. Each time it happened, the principal called a conference with our parents and the offended teacher, trying to "work things out." I, on the other hand, thought I could be accepted by trying to be perfect and liked by all.

Taller than all of the girls in my class and most of the boys, and with skin the color of a brown paper bag, fitting in quickly turned into an impossible goal. My looks didn't conform to any American standard of beauty in those days. One had to be blond, blue-eyed, and bubbly or Mediterranean and sultry like Annette Funicello of *The Mickey Mouse Club* to get noticed. Yet I dreamed, against all probability, of being considered beautiful. Swans became my favorite creatures at the zoo because of how the Ugly Duckling turned into the most prized of the lot after suffering through a difficult youth. I also hungered to be part of a community with other little "colored" children (who looked like me) and daydreamed about a tall, dark, handsome, and sophisticated suitor who one day would sweep me off to faraway places with strange-sounding names. From the way I wallflower-papered the gym at school mixers, becoming attractive seemed just as improbable as finding my mesmerizing knight. The few backhanded compliments I did get ("I like Gail because I like dark meat") made my stomach turn.

My brother and I had to attend daily Mass, study catechism, and participate in church activities, so we both, eventually, succumbed to the weight of it and changed religions. We wanted to be more like our classmates, although I think David had more of a "calling" for Catholicism and even discussed the priesthood with his high school counselor. I remember screaming hysterically when he told us of his ambition. Although we fought constantly, he was still my big brother and I loved him. I was afraid I'd never see him again. I, too, had moments of religious fervor. I especially liked to make novenas. Only nine days of prayers and candle lighting could get me my heart's desire. Not a bad deal. Once I almost burned up my room during a novena, but anything was worth making my fantasies come true. Plus, "becoming a convert" carried a certain cachet at school, and the nuns announced our decision almost reverentially. Converts were special because we had made a choice to join those who had been "chosen," or something like that. Some of the dogma did not make much sense to me but whenever I questioned it, I got the "company" line. "That is subject to faith, and you must take it on faith."

My father didn't help much, being an infrequent churchgoer and a fairly rational sort. I remember his explaining to me, as a nine- or ten-year-old, how everything that was on the earth when it came into being was still here. It had just changed form. Apple seeds turn into trees that bear fruit and so on. I got the picture. He said that there was only one exception. "When the Russians sent up Sputniks outside the earth's atmosphere. You see, they can't come back to the earth." "And the Virgin Mary," I added. He looked at me long and hard.

"That's what the nuns over there at that school are teaching you, are they?"

I nodded dutifully, and he said nothing. But I knew in my bones that he wasn't buying it. Even one of the parish priests increased my skepticism. Maybe he and my father were in cahoots:

"I didn't say my prayers three times this week," I once disclosed during confession.

"What did you say?" the voice from behind the screen queried.

I repeated my sin.

"Is that what the nuns are telling you is a sin? Well, don't listen to everything they say," he counseled me.

On the face of it, I was well liked. Part of the most popular clique at the school, I edged my way in by giving more than I got. And I had more to give because my parents were wealthier than any of the other parents. The parties they put together for my classmates were the best. We had all of the trimmings and then some, including movies since my father had a top-of-the-line Bell & Howell motion picture camera and projector. My parents would borrow cartoons and short movies from the public library, to everyone's delight. Our favorite was one where a family of greenhorn campers is no match for a family of bears who knock over and lick the contents of every jar or bottle they can get their paws on. My friends never tired of it, and they always looked forward to our annual showing of the bears wreaking havoc on the campsite.

Nonetheless, my friendships had their limits. When school let out and the St. Louis weather turned to fire and brimstone, kids hightailed it to the nearest swimming pool. Cannonballing into a large body of deep water was about the only way to combat the impossibly humid heat. Public accommodations acts were spreading across the country, and by 1961, St. Louis had one on the books. But which swimming pool conformed to the new legislation and which did not was anyone's guess. Some pools attempted to get around the law by going "private," although any white person could become a member on a daily basis for a trifle.

So, my Catholic school friends and I would plan to go swimming. I would wait for the final details but they never came. I telephoned their homes to hear that they had already left. I remember sitting at home on those days, staring out the window, and wondering what happened. I soon found out. They would call from someone's backyard or a picnic ground or swimming pool. Laughingly, they would tell me about how much fun they were having and how they had forgotten to telephone. Not even the blistering St. Louis sunshine singed me as much as their trickery. Was it because I was colored and might be refused admittance, or was it because they were jealous of the material "things" I had that their parents couldn't afford? Maybe it was the town car from my grandparents' funeral home that occasionally picked us up on Friday afternoons that sent my friends over the edge. Probably a combination of all of these things, but I never asked because my father's words would ring in my ears whenever I thought about confronting them.

"Remember, you have to be smarter and stronger than white folks. And don't ever let them see the pain they inflict 'cause then they'll know how to get at you," he chided. I think they had figured out how to get under my skin because my silence certainly didn't stop them. And I kept falling for it. I guess I hoped that they really had just forgotten to call.

I took the matter into my own hands during one of St. Louis's normal, scorchingly hot summers. I suggested we all go to a public pool I knew I could get into. Because it was located even farther south than where most of us lived, my father would drive us. He walked us to the entrance to make sure there was, in fact, no hitch. Even though I was with my friends, I wished for one of my camouflaged days. I hoped that, among a sea of white faces, I could pass through the turnstile, change in the dressing room, slip into the pool to escape the blasted St. Louis heat, and retrace my steps without being seen. I was only fooling myself.

At some point while I was alone, three boys cornered me and looked me over. "What are you? An Indian?" one said. Then pausing, he shouted, "Or a nigger?" All of the blood in my body rushed to my head, along with my roaring heartbeat, and I froze. They stepped closer and the same one said it again, but this time more menacingly, "Well, what are you? An Indian or a nigger?" All I could think of was how to get them to leave me alone. "I'm an Indian," I almost whispered, and, mollified, they walked away. I may have come with friends, but I honestly don't remember being with anyone. All I'm sure of was that when I told that lie, I felt as if I had betrayed my entire race. And one day I'd have to pay heavy dues. St. Peter might extract them from me, but I would have to pay!

When my father dropped off the last of my friends later that afternoon, he noted my somber mood and asked me what was wrong. "I told a lie, Daddy."

"What about?" he said without taking his eyes off the road. I explained what happened, and he started to laugh.

"That's all right. You outfoxed them," he said, when he finished the laugh that I didn't understand.

"But I lied!"

"Now let me tell you something about lying. There's a right time to lie and a not-so-right time to lie."

He then told me a story about himself and one of his childhood friends, Herb Duckett, who had worked on the soft coal issue with Ray Tucker, who was, by now, St. Louis's mayor. Daddy and Herb had grown up together in St. Louis and were born within a few years of each other. They were both too young to serve in World War I and too old for World War II, although my father tried, as a fifteen-year-old, to lie himself into the first one. That lie, he admitted, had been a virtuous yet stupid one.

This tale took place in 1942—wartime. They were at the Kansas City train station, having just arrived from St. Louis. Both almost forty years old, but still feeling and acting like pups, they strutted through the terminal.

"Hey, boys, shouldn't you be gettin' on a train outta here? KC's got all the niggers we need," rang out anonymously.

Daddy and Herb stopped in their tracks, pivoted around, and began searching the station for the person attached to the voice. They saw a white man, barely in his twenties, rolling up his sleeves, clenching his fists, and beckoning them to fight. He was backed up by about a dozen white men who were beginning to form a circle around my father and Herb. Instinctively, they stood back to back and balled up their hands. But then my father began shouting into the crowd:

"How dare you? A Negro can't even walk into a public place without being humiliated, but we sure as hell can send our boys off to the killing fields of Europe so you can feel safe and sound here at home. I've lost not one, but BOTH OF MY SONS, you hear me, in this war of yours."

He almost choked up and then stopped his outburst. At that point, the white men relaxed their fists and the circle began to dissolve. Hightailing it to the hills oftentimes being the better part of valor, my father and Herb took their leave promptly, with heads up and chests out. Once outside the station, they darted around the corner.

"Dave, where in the hell did you come up with that lie?" Herb asked.

"Man, it was lying time!"

He explained to me that not only was he divorced and childless at the time, but Negro soldiers hadn't yet seen any combat. But what did white folks know about that? The armed services were still segregated then. Daddy had lost a nephew in the war, however, at Pearl Harbor, and may have unconsciously invoked his memory in Kansas City. Named after my father, he, too, had wanted to "see the world" and, passing for white, enlisted in the navy. Daddy still got so tickled by telling this story, one that I would hear over and over for years, that his laugh shook his sizable belly and broad shoulders as he drove home. And this time, I laughed along with him. He then told me, "If anyone ever asks you again what you are, just say that you're an American."

Fitting into my neighborhood outside of grade school was, in many ways, a bigger hurdle. We lived three blocks from Grand Avenue, a main thoroughfare that ran the full length of the city from north to south. The part of the street closest to our house was lined with grocery and convenience stores, clothing shops, cleaners, restaurants, a bank, a pharmacy, movie house, and a five-and-dime store that still added ½ cents to its prices and gave change with red mills (coins worth $\frac{1}{10}$ of a cent). I entered most of these establishments without incident, except when I wanted to eat a meal or see a film. I never knew if I would be confronted by "unknowing," as I came to think of it.

As soon as I entered certain coffee shops or diners with my white friends, I remember waitresses in starched uniforms glaring down at me, hesitating for an instant, and then authoritatively stating, "We don't serve colored." This was my cue to get out. Sometimes my white companions left with me, and sometimes they didn't. Not that it made any difference since nothing could compensate for the loneliness I felt in that moment. As I left, I tried to keep my chin up as my parents did when confronting Jim Crow; sometimes I managed to and other times I didn't. I wanted to run down the nearest alley, dive into the trash cans, and cry my eyes out. Instead, I just walked away, while my ears rang hollow and my face burned cold. Those four words represented an unseen barrier between me and the rest of the world until I heard the comeback that Herb used to turn the tables. "Glad to hear that because I don't eat them. But I'll take some bacon and eggs."

Going to the movies turned out to be a more unpredictable trial. Sometimes I got in, and sometimes I didn't. My father was irate when my mother, brother, and I were refused admission once and, in league with one of the parish priests, launched a campaign against the theater. It worked because I usually got a ticket after that. "Unknowing" sometimes still awaited me, especially if I went to a different neighborhood movie house.

I don't remember the names of many of the films from the late '50s and early '60s. Elvis Presley musicals, the romantic comedies set on California beaches, Westerns, and movies about white college students going to Florida on spring break seemed to dominate the screens—nothing I could identify with, for sure. The only one that had anything to do with Negroes was notorious, and was only talked about in whispers around my neighborhood; I never saw it. The poster showed a downtrodden-looking woman and a man with his back to her. I can't remember the name of the movie but the taglines were something like, "No Shame Could Be Worse than This!" and "You'll Be Shocked!" It was the story of a white couple who had a black baby. It turned out that the wife had a Negro relative she knew nothing about. It frightened a lot of people since they worried about the horror of something similar coming their way.

I usually didn't tell my parents about being refused service in the restaurants. In those days, it would have been futile. I had seen how they had been denied at a local restaurant. One of the best seafood eateries in town, Edmonds, was only a stone's throw from our house. My parents could call in our order, walk in the front door, pick it up, and leave. So I figured that my being turned away would doubly infuriate them. Their child was singled out because of the way she looked and they couldn't do much about it. But even before the law changed, there were a few white restaurants in other parts of town that gladly welcomed us. I remember going to my first nightclub, the Black Angus, for surf 'n' turf, although I didn't know it was called that then, and to Nantucket Cove for seafood. My parents went to the Crystal Palace in Gaslight Square, whose owners felt that anyone who could pay their prices was welcome.

My father's temper scared me at times. I had witnessed his hazel eyes grow steely, his jaws tighten, and his rage rise whenever we encountered racism on the south side. As a result, I sometimes didn't tell him about everything that happened. Yet there were exceptions. One evening the front door bell rang. Outside of Halloween and whenever my parents had a party, almost no one came to our house at night. It was a teenage boy from the neighborhood who had been injured in a car accident and needed a lawyer. My mother answered the door and, remembering how lucrative personal injury cases could be, she quickly guided him into our living room and ran upstairs to get my father. As I peered over the railing from the upstairs landing, all I could hear was "NIGGER, NIGGER, NIGGER." He seemed to know only that word whenever he saw me, and I always tried to dodge him on the street. He would chase me on foot or with his bicycle until he grew bored—or until I managed to plaster myself against a gangway wall and lose him. My brother had even defended me in a fistfight with him once, but lost. His rival was big for his age and David was not.

Before Daddy could make it down the stairs, I blurted out the backstory as fast as I could. "You stay upstairs," he instructed me. "I'll take care of this." He descended those steps as if he were marching in one of those long-ago picket lines and proceeded to give the boy a verbal flogging. After Daddy finished, the boy said, "Mr. Grant, I'm real sorry about what I did and I promise I won't do it again, but will you be my lawyer?" It was the ultimate vindication—an apology, an acknowledgment of my father's reputation, AND legal fees to boot! "And that's the way she [sometimes] goes."

My parents always emphasized that none of this Jim Crow nonsense was our fault. We weren't treated this way because we were inferior or deserving of any abuse. White people had the problem! To me, they seemed to have had the biggest difficulty with more than momentary contact with us. I guess they interpreted it as socializing with colored. We could buy clothes or groceries and leave the white owner's store. It was rather a fear of any sort of prolonged closeness to us. Sitting next to us at a restaurant or movie theater certainly qualified. And they certainly weren't going to allow their barely clothed bodies in a swimming pool with similarly scantily clad Negroes. In those days, the ultimate expression of their mania would follow them to the grave. In order to ensure that they did not have to be near us for a really, really long time, cemeteries were segregated as well.

Before restaurants and the like started to open up to all St. Louisans, I remember how we contented ourselves with Sunday afternoon excursions to Lambert Field, St. Louis's airport. It took almost an hour to get there from Arsenal Street, twice the amount of time it now takes, but the ride was worth it. We'd watch propeller planes take off and land. We could walk right out on the field to a concession that sold snacks and ice-cold drinks (some kind of orange soda, as I remember it) from a tall glass container, shaped like a globe.

The highlight of such free and available-to-all events came in early December when we waited for twilight so we could pile in our car, head downtown, and walk from one major department store to the next for the brightly lit Christmas window decorations. Sometimes we'd join with other families and rent a cabin on Kentucky Lake, near Paducah, for Thanksgiving or for a week or two in summer. We could go to any circus that passed through town and stand on the sidelines during parades, although I never got too near the Columbus Day Parade that snaked through our neighborhood for fear of being called the "word." I always felt that our parents did their best to entertain us as children, but Jim Crow put limits on them.

I found it so strange that my parents chose to be marooned on the humdrum south side when most of the action, as I imagined it, lay north. Besides exchanging formalities, they certainly didn't socialize with anyone in our neighborhood. It would take decades before I figured out how much courage it instilled in me. In the meantime, I coped, ignoring as much as I could, while I dreamed about my errant knight.

After I finished elementary school, my commute to high school became much shorter. My parents enrolled me in a Catholic all-girls academy, less than a block from our home. A different kind of "unknowing" awaited me there. Almost immediately, a pudgy, pint-sized nun took it upon herself to take me under her habit, which was difficult since I was about six inches taller than she. She told me, in all sincerity, what was expected during my years at the academy:

"You must be a credit to your race," she said with determination.

I didn't know what she meant exactly but interpreted this as having to get excellent grades, always be on time and obedient, and, primarily, not to have any fun. She reinforced my understanding of what she expected, with a raised eyebrow or disapproving stare as she tucked her arms inside the flap of her gown, whenever I crossed the line she had drawn for me. I got plenty of unpleasant looks because I only managed to fulfill her last unspoken order.

There was one place in the neighborhood, a diner, where my friends and I did escape after school to have some "fun." Strictly off limits to us (full of Protestants and smoke, the nuns warned us), we would sneak there and hope we didn't get caught in one of the sisters' stealth raids on the "joint." I especially wanted to go because I couldn't be refused service since the public accommodations bill was being enforced by now. And the hamburgers and shakes were legendary.

The nuns chastised some of my classmates when they were spotted in the bakery two doors from my house. I had breakfast at home and was always running late so I never joined them there. As hard as we tried, we could never figure out what was threatening about doughnuts and Danish—too much sugar, maybe?

The thing I most dreaded was when my "protector" called me to her office for a talk:

"You're not being a credit to your race. And remember, you MUST be a credit to your race."

The one thing I never understood was what she knew about my race or what she knew about being a credit to it. I was one of only six colored girls out of a student population of more than five hundred. It wasn't about being a credit to my people, I soon realized, but rather about validating the sisters' decision to admit me in the first place. They certainly didn't want to be "embarrassed." I knew I had to be "smarter and stronger and better" than white folks, according to my father, but that was for survival. My "race," that is, my family and their friends, already thought I was pretty terrific.

I did manage to serve in many elected positions throughout high school, including as senior class president, the first Negro to do so, which was duly noted in the local newspapers along with my photo as proof of my race. I felt that was a credit to my parents. By so doing, I became, for my chubby albatross, a true credit to my race. She meant well; she just didn't know what she meant.

12.

What a Pair!

*I*N OUR RATHER MONOTONOUS NEIGHBORHOOD, THERE
was no way my parents could blend in. My mother was
glamorous and sophisticated to me, in complete contrast to the
mothers of my playmates. I knew all about her high schooling in
California and college in Chicago. She'd even traveled extensively
in the United States and to Mexico and Canada before marrying
my father. She always said that besides marrying our father and
having us, living in San Diego was the happiest time in her life.

I can't think of one thing my parents had in common with
our neighbors, other than concern for their children. But even
then, their interests diverged. My mother and father wanted to
protect us as much as possible from the consequences of racism
and, for them, higher and higher education was the key. They
wanted to ensure that I, as the girl, was prepared to make a living with or without a husband. The neighbors just wanted their
daughters to get married and their sons to get a decent-paying job
with benefits right after high school. Besides the racial chasm that
separated them, there was a major "what's it all about" breach.

My parents were considered one of the most striking couples in town, and heads turned wherever they went. They were both headstrong, independent, and charismatic. The St. Louis dowagers and pundits alike agreed that their marriage would never last. Forty years later when my father died in the home where I grew up, my mother was at his side and still married to him. As a child, I was in awe of them both. But sometimes I secretly wished that they would not stick out as much as they did in our neighborhood.

Before my mother stopped working in my father's office, we had several different nursemaids who looked after us during the day, another oddity for our neighborhood. One of our first housekeepers was a spectacled, hefty woman who wore a starched white apron and sturdy walking shoes in the summer, and she never left the house without her mink-trimmed coat when the weather turned cold. She took another job when I was a toddler, and I only know her from photos. Mrs. Borum, my favorite, replaced her and worked at our home through my teen years. Unfailingly on the lookout, she rarely let me out of her sight until second or third grade, holding my hand when I wanted to go to the candy store three doors away. When she finally got tired of listening to my complaints about being old enough to go there alone, she would plant herself in front of our house and watch me walk there, and wait until I came back. She played gospel music for us on the radio when our parents went out and she babysat us. I am embarrassed to say that my brother and I didn't always appreciate this. Our teasing, however, never put the slightest dent in her love for us and she'd just laugh us off. I also learned what vitiligo was from Mrs. Borum, as she steadily lost her deep brown pigmentation and turned into a woman covered with egg-white patches of skin. She was one of the most sincere people I've ever known.

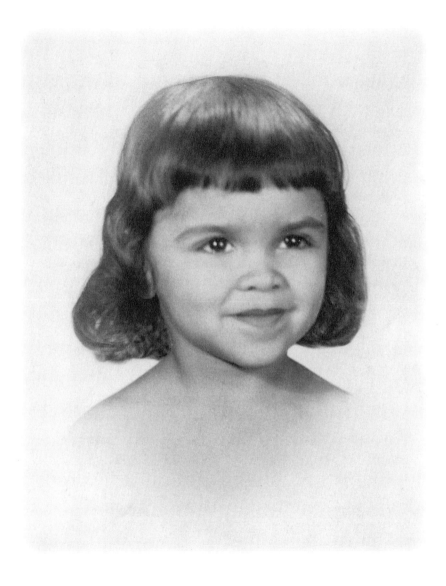

Gail Milissa Grant, 1953.

My parents' social life took place on the north side with other professional families. My father belonged to the Royal Vagabonds, whose annual New Year's Eve party was still "fabulous," the event of the holiday season. My mother shied away from girls' clubs, such as the Links or the Girl Friends. These were national clubs with local chapters and founded largely as social outlets for their members. The meetings were held in their homes (where else?), and each Girl Friend or Link made sure everything (from table service to linens to food and drink) reflected only the best in taste. Mommy was never much of a joiner, unless it involved a tour group headed off to South America or the Caribbean.

The other side of town, which represented a mere four- or five-mile trek, was a world apart to me. While most of my friendships developed closer to home, I played with some of the children of my parents' circle. They all seemed so bold and sure of themselves. They had their own social clubs, like Jack and Jill and Tots and Teens; used slang that I didn't understand; and were fairly content to inhabit a segregated north side where the world was, indeed, their oyster. Next to them, I felt like Ollie B., my mother's country cousin, who visited us once from Tennessee and arrived with his suitcase tied shut with heavy cord. Or were his pants held up with it? Or both? I didn't realize that being the color of a brown paper bag with borderline aquiline features and flyaway, curly hair scored big beauty points in "their" world. If I had, I might have spent less time wishing to be a swan.

My mother bought some of our groceries by going north, and I loved riding with her through streets jammed with activity. She sought out the soul food that our local stores didn't carry. She purchased fresh catfish and crappie from open-air stalls, as well as collard and mustard greens, bulbous turnips on stems that seemed as tall as me, and pigs' feet, snoots, and ham hocks. She also shopped at downtown's Union Market, where she had gone with her mother as a child. While there, we sometimes went shopping at one of the big department stores and had lunch in its cafeteria. Usually the only Negroes in sight, we were riding just behind the crest of a wave that would soon wash over America. Whites were not yet ready to get wet. Talking ceased when we entered, but the stares never did. A family friend happened by once while we were eating and he summed up what must have been on everyone else's mind in the restaurant. He slid into a seat at our table, leaned back, crossed his legs, surveyed the scene, cocked one eye, and said, "I bet I know what all of these white people are wondering. What in the world is this Caucasian woman doing here with a Mexican child and that Negro man?" I laughed along with my mother, not fully understanding the joke but questioning why he would call me a Mexican when I knew I wasn't.

My mother's Caucasian cast never affected me until I left St. Louis. Outside of my hometown, people didn't know my mother wasn't white and would sometimes assume she was when she visited me. I spoke English properly, was educated, and knew how to deal with most people—nothing terribly outlandish or noteworthy, having been raised squarely in middle-class America. Yet when viewed by some white people, these fundamentals became so outstanding that they must have been the result "of a white parent." I always wanted to introduce her by saying, "and by the way, she's not white." Their satisfied looks bothered me: "Aha, I just knew she had a white parent. No wonder she is so well spoken, so well whatever. So much like us." The truth eventually came out, and I guess it was worth the wait; they were even more puzzled.

My mother may have stopped working for my father in the early 1950s, but she didn't stop helping support our family. She became licensed as a real estate broker, and I remember her throwing us in the back of her four-seater Nash Rambler and speeding off to show properties to her clients. David and I always found something to fight about along the way. "King" of the coveted padded armrest in the back seat was our most frequent battle. It flipped up or down, and whoever controlled it won, which meant knocking each other off it repeatedly.

My mother always had household help, was svelte and immaculately groomed, and read about faraway places with strange-sounding names. My father called her "Red" for her auburn locks and freckles, and my brother nicknamed her "Bubbles" one day and captured the effervescence of her personality. As far back as I can remember, she took us on weekend trips to Chicago to see our great aunts when school was in session and on longer visits in the summers. She drove us cross-country several times to Los Angeles on Route 66's two-lane highway. Both of these destinations were like the Promised Land to me. It felt as if we could go anywhere—to restaurants and stores and movies and the beaches—without the stress of "unknowing" hovering over me.

We did have a scrape with it once, however, on our way to the West Coast when we were refused service at a diner in Oklahoma City. I remember how my mother walked into the place—as if she owned it—and the way she left it when it was clear that she didn't—the same way she had come in. She was boiling mad but she just got in the car and went to the next restaurant she could find and entered it the same way. As the hostess pulled three menus from behind her station, my mother told her what had just happened to us. The white woman blushed and said something like, "I'm so sorry. We're not like that here," and escorted us to a table. I'm not certain but I think we got our desserts on the house.

Los Angeles had many colorful neighborhoods to explore: Olvera Street where we gorged on enchiladas and tacos, tried on sombreros, and listened to strolling Mexican musicians; Chinatown with its restaurants and curio shops; the Farmers Market—an enormous, covered, outdoor shopping mall that flaunted California's wealth of produce for the world to see; and numerous black communities with all sorts, sizes, and shades of stucco homes and flats, some with swimming pools. The best excursions were to Knott's Berry Farm, America's first theme park, and the newly opened Disneyland.

Chicago was as engaging but in a different way. Its South Side still had almost everything the larger white community had. Full of upscale businesses and theaters, one could live a lifetime within its borders. No weekend trip was complete until we had Sunday brunch at the top of the then-tallest structure downtown—the Prudential Building. No summer was satisfying until we rode every ride at the integrated Riverview Amusement Park. I don't remember ever attending the park's famous "Midnight Ramble," when the grounds were taken over by Chicago's colored kids, but I felt as if I had. It was the high point of my friends' summer and they described it in such detail that I got a rush just listening to them. It ran from 8:00 p.m. until midnight with no parents in sight!

St. Louis had its own Riverview, also known as Chain of Rocks Amusement Park, on the far north side of town. I went there at least once but recall feeling nervous. It carried its own "unknowing" baggage, marked as it was by whites' rioting when the park was integrated around 1950 and by further periodic outbreaks of violence thereafter. The Forest Park Highlands was the city's largest and best-known amusement park—and segregated. It may have let down the bars to us before it closed in 1967, but given its reputation I never went on any of its rides. Built on twenty-three acres of land, it stretched for what seemed like a mile along one of the city's major thoroughfares. Riding past it with the windows rolled down, I could hear the children's laughter as they bumped each other in the dodge 'em cars or their screams as they rode the Comet, the park's roller coaster. I always wondered what it would be like to ride on it, a twisting mountain of a ride that looked like it was made of gigantic matchsticks. I did go to the Highlands's swimming pool—just once and just before it closed—without incident. Yet Chicago's Riverview held my affection. I knew it had its share of racial incidents but I never experienced them. A little on the raucous side, to me it was the world's best joyride.

While in Chicago, we usually stayed with one of our great aunts. Each would try to outdo the other by packing a homemade lunch for us to take on the road back home so we wouldn't have to tiptoe around restaurants that might not serve us. They usually mimicked one another's menu and stuck to fried chicken, potato salad, and deviled eggs, with salt and pepper separately wrapped in waxed-paper wedges. Aunt Clara, who had married again and moved back to Chicago, specialized in baking bread and, if she felt like it, would include a warm loaf, tucked inside a linen towel. Aunt Bert had her own recipe for dinner rolls that had to be torn apart from each other; when we did, the butter almost dripped from the edges. So they did do battle in the bread department. Or they may have just slathered butter on slices of bread from the Butternut Bakery, a wholesaler that had a retail entrance. I always imagined that the residents who lived around the bakery might have stormed the place if they couldn't buy its goods—the impossibly delicious smell of its freshly baked bread wafted for blocks in all directions. We usually only stopped by to see Aunt Minnie. She was one of the first-born Franklins and her days of fixing elaborate meals were over, although she would still have a peach or blackberry cobbler waiting for us.

I actually got to know these great aunts much better than any of my grandparents, since they outlived them all by decades. Daddy's father died when he was thirteen, and his mother passed in 1955, just as I turned six years old. I had to rely on my parents' stories about their parents for an understanding of how hard they worked to create their businesses and educate their families. Grandpa and Grandma Hughes had come from Tennessee with only grade school educations; my father's father had finished high school, but Madam Grant hadn't.

Aunt Minnie Franklin Ware, ca. 1930. Courtesy of the Moorland-Spingarn Research Center, Howard University, Washington, D.C., Mildred H. Grant Collection.

Before her death, Grandmother Grant and Aunt Vivian occasionally came to our house for dinner. Usually dressed in a black, ankle-length dress, Madam Grant looked at me tenderly but still seemed fairly unapproachable, although my mother claimed she had a great sense of humor. Vivian, with her barely noticeable smile and dark-rimmed, downcast eyes, rarely spoke at table, except to her mother or my father. Many of my parents' friends talked to me about Madam Grant and how respected she was in the community, and how much I physically resembled her. They also spoke of Vivian, underscoring that she wasn't pitiable, just limited. (Vivian died five years after her mother.) After Grandmother Grant's death, my parents took me to one of the houses where she had worked on Lindell Boulevard. I believe it was the Anheuser mansion. Dressed in my Sunday best, I met some of the family. They seemed to know my father well, with first names exchanged all around. My grandmother, however, was still Madam Grant to them and they were delighted to meet her granddaughter. I don't remember what they said about her; among other sights, I was transfixed on the massive chandelier that crowned their private ballroom.

The Hugheses were still having wakes and funerals, albeit few, by the time I remember going to the visit them on Lawton Avenue. The heart of the house remained in the kitchen with its oblong dining table and the miniscule sink whose tap marked "cold" spewed hot water and vice versa. They'd been that way forever, and no one thought to switch them around. Grandma would still handily prepare meals with my mother assisting her. Grandpa was failing. He walked with a cane but would always make his appearance at the wake, lean against the back wall for a respectable period, hobble upstairs, and then descend in time to bid everyone farewell. They had "help" only as needed but always seemed to have a chauffeur on hand. I doubt that either of them ever drove themselves anywhere. David and I treated as our own, Mother's long-ago favorite plaything—the church truck. One of us would stretch out on its cool stainless-steel top and pretend to be in flight while the other would push.

Our grandparents' mood visibly improved whenever we were around. "Would you like some big man's coffee with breakfast?" my grandmother crooned to my brother and me in the morning. A brew of hot water, warm cream, and sugar, it was how she satisfied our pleas to drink real coffee just like the grown-ups did. She always served it to us in oversized coffee cups on saucers and never in anything that resembled a mug. This tradition would follow us to Arsenal Street, where mugs never lined our kitchen cabinets. I would not learn the touching significance of this practice until decades after Grandma passed away and someone asked me why I didn't have any mugs on my shelves.

Grandpa Hughes died about a month after Grandmother Grant; a year or two later, Grandma Hughes was diagnosed with cancer. In the meantime, I do recall several excursions with her—once when her driver took us to the Union Market to buy groceries. I met all of the vendors she'd known for decades, especially the butcher. He still treated her as a special customer. "I've got a great cut of meat for you, Mrs. Hughes," he said. "I've been holding it aside for you." Another time, she took me shopping at one of the fancy department stores downtown and bought me a midnight blue, felt hoop skirt with pink poodles stitched onto it. Then she got really sick. My father raised more than a little Cain when she was put in the basement of Barnes Hospital. He threatened to run for his Bell & Howell camera and film the exposed pipes and beams over her head, but she was swiftly taken to an aboveground floor.

She and her hospital bed moved into my bedroom as the cancer took over, and both David and I relocated to the third floor until she died. My most lingering memories are of her inescapable screams in the night when her pain became unbearable, and of her lethargy during the daylight hours. Aunt Clara and Aunt Bert helped my mother care for Grandma during the last months of her life. They took turns visiting from Chicago—a week here, a week there. After Grandma passed, these two immediately took over as our grandmothers. They savored the new part they played in our lives. Just as they had nurtured our mother in San Diego and Chicago during her schooling, they now had her children to mind. They did their best to make up for our lacking the mothers and fathers of our parents.

They also became my friends and confidantes for decades. Aunt Clara taught me a lot of practical things. She told me to rotate the bed linens each time I changed them so they would wear evenly. She once scolded me when I almost tossed an eggshell before inserting my pinkie into it and scraping out the last bit of white for the cake we were making together. "You're wasting half the egg," she said. She then showed me how to get it all out. Then as I stood there beating the batter clockwise and my arm grew tired, I changed directions and turned it counterclockwise. "Don't back-beat that cake. You'll ruin it!" she said. I didn't even know she was watching me since she was intensely glued to her job of grating fresh coconut for the icing. When we finished, she crushed the eggshells, led me to her garden, and showed me how to scatter them as fertilizer. When Aunt Bert's second husband died, she used to call me and we'd gossip about her new boyfriend. My aunts were warm and funny and wonderful.

We sometimes drove east during the summer to visit my godparents, the Calloways, who lived in a big white house on almost

Aunt Bertha Franklin Penny, ca. 1925. Courtesy of the Moorland-Spingarn Research Center, Howard University, Washington, D.C., Mildred H. Grant Collection.

two acres of land in Westchester County, New York. There was another kind of "unknowing" I felt out east—a sort of, "How am I supposed to act amongst all these very sophisticated, good-looking, famous black people?"

Aunt Clara Robinson, date unknown.

One trip, however, distinguished itself from all of the others. In the summer of 1954, my parents and I went to Cuba to visit Uncle Cab and his family while he performed in Havana for a month. My brother didn't come because he was ensconced at his annual summer retreat—Camp Don Bosco for Boys—and refused to budge. I remember all of the preparations for our drive from St. Louis to Miami, where we would board a ship for Havana. My parents plotted out our itinerary with the help of the famed TripTiks from the Automobile Association of America. Once that was done, they telephoned people they knew who lived along the route, asking if we could overnight with them. They also called their St. Louis network for names of friends or family who would host us. It seemed like an escapade to me; I never realized just how serious, and potentially dangerous, the going and coming parts of our vacation would be. We were driving through the South—a land filled with more "unknowing" than anywhere in America at the time. Each of my parents' friends concluded their conversation with the same advice: "And remember, if you have to stop for the night where you don't know anyone, go to the local preacher or undertaker. You'll usually find them on the other side of the railroad tracks. One of them should be able to tell you where there's someplace that accepts colored—a roadhouse, or motel, or room to rent in someone's house."

I mainly recall the whimsy of the weeping willow trees, the scorching southern sunshine, and the poisonous spider I found inside the chest of drawers at one of the places we stayed on the other side of the tracks. Beauty, heat, and danger—that summed up the South for me as a child until we reached Miami, where we were welcomed royally at the legendary Lord Calvert Hotel. It catered to well-off blacks and was more like a motel with all of the rooms surrounding an inner courtyard and pool. Ella Fitzgerald was one of the guests. We left for Havana late one afternoon just as the sun kissed the horizon and we arrived in its harbor the next morning. Uncle Cab met us and pushed his way past the horde of Cubans on the pier, all chirping "Cab Calloway, Cab

David M. Grant, Gail Milissa Grant, and Mildred Grant en route to
Havana, Cuba, at the Lord Calvert Hotel, Miami, Florida, ca. 1953.

Calloway, Cab Calloway." A sensation in Havana, Uncle Cab was
surrounded by crowds wherever he went.

We spent several weeks with him and his family at the bun-
galow he had rented. My father and I would awake at dawn and
wander along the retaining wall that kept the sea at bay in downtown Havana. I recall the primary colors of the clothes that the
women wore, the friendliness of all the Cubans we met, and Ful-
gencio Batista's soldiers with bazookas slung over their shoulders.
Havana had its own brand of beauty, warmth, and danger. We

retraced our steps on the return home, sidestepping the roadhouse with the spiders. We, however, did get stranded one more time on this trip. Our friends' advice could not tell us which gas station to sidestep. When we filled up the tank at one, and my mother tried to use the bathroom, she was "refused service." "What am I supposed to do," she snapped at the attendant as she thrust her cupped hands in his face, "pee here?"

Ordinarily, my father wasn't too much of a traveler, but he enjoyed our Cuban getaway and he liked going back east to visit his friends in Washington and New York. He loved being an attorney and was always itching to get back to court. He was the only dad around our neighborhood who wore a suit and tie to work and who drove there each morning in a late-model car. He usually rose before dawn and descended to the basement where he stoked the furnace with coal, sometimes with our help, until we changed over to oil heat. He then two-finger-tapped out court motions on a typewriter or wrote legal briefs in longhand. I saw him as a funny, affectionate man with a big stomach who sometimes held me captive as he told me about his latest trial in court or quoted legal precedents. His appearance, however, belied a steely character. The stories told time and again gave me a glimpse of the relentless duel he had carried on with St. Louis's power structure over equality for Negroes under the law for nearly two decades before my birth. Fortunately, I also witnessed some of his derring-do, firsthand.

When I was about seven or eight years old, my father was arrested for the last time in his life. I was away at summer camp and I heard about it on the radio. Fortunately, by the time the news reached me, he had already been released and was at home. All I knew was that he had been arrested for something having to do with a license plate.

Earlier that summer my father bought a Cadillac, second-hand, from one of his friends who traded hers in every year or two for the newest model. He'd never owned this make, preferring Chevrolets, but she gave him a good deal, and he decided to splurge a little this time. He was driving home at twilight and had just crossed Chouteau Avenue when the police pulled him over and told him they couldn't read his rear license plate. Cadillacs had electric lights that illuminated the plates but, according to them, the numbers were smudged. Furthermore, they told him to open the trunk because they wanted to search it. He refused since they had no cause and no search warrant. He also declined to take the ticket and became belligerent, just hoping they would arrest him on this trumped-up charge; they did. He then secretly smiled to himself because he knew where they would take him and who would be in charge of the station.

When the police escorted my dad into the precinct and the captain appeared at the desk, he screamed out at the cops: "What have you done? Do you know who this is?" He then went into a tirade about how this would be all over the news and how damaging the publicity would be to the police force, and so on. When he finished, my father only added, "You got that right!" He and the captain could already envision the headline: "David M. Grant, Prominent Negro Attorney and Civil Rights Activist, Arrested for an Obstructed License Plate." And the news hit the papers just about like that, much to the City's embarrassment. At least for a while, Negroes didn't get pulled over for no reason. "And that's the way she goes."

Around the same time as this incident, Daddy created a furor that caused us to take an unplanned, lickety-split vacation. My father was elected in 1956 as one of thirteen members of the Board of Freeholders to write a new city charter. He later talked about how Jordan Chambers had hand-selected him to run, knowing he could win. Because it was an unpaid position, my father objected at first. "Jordan, I got two kids I got late in life. I've got to educate them. I just don't have that kind of time." Jordan bit down hard on his cigar and said, "All those reasons are personal, aren't they?" My dad said yes. "Well, this one's got to pass your personal consideration; this one you owe the people." He then stroked my father's ego but also spoke the truth: "You tell me somebody who knows as much about municipal government as you know, and who'll speak and take a stand like you will, and I'll let you off the hook." With that reasoning and after my father ran it past my mother, he was now 100 percent hooked! He ran fourth in a field of more than forty and immediately became chair of the Committee on Legislation. He worked longer hours than usual because of the charter and his legal practice. He'd come home exhausted, but I also recall how energized he was as a freeholder. He felt that, most probably, he wouldn't leave us a large inheritance but by having his name on a city charter that could last for decades, he would leave us a more meaningful legacy.

Well, it didn't quite turn out that way because the powers that be saw to it that the new charter would dilute black voting power and reduce Negro representation on the Board of Aldermen. Daddy refused to sign the charter, and the city fathers fumed. So angry were they, in fact, that we got in a car and skedaddled to Indiana on an abruptly arranged vacation. When we came back, my father and other black politicians organized a grassroots campaign to defeat the charter, and they did—with blacks casting decisive votes. Some credit this victory with awakening the St. Louis black community to its electoral power. Before long, there were two more black aldermen, a black on the school board, and Ted McNeal as the first black in the Missouri Senate.

Left to right: St. Louis School Board member James Hurt, State Senator Theodore D. McNeal, Eighteenth Ward committeeman Fred Weathers, Jordan Chambers, and David M. Grant, ca. 1960.

Shortly after the freeholder debacle, the Board of Aldermen created a position for my father—as director of legislative research. "Keep your friends close and your enemies closer." I think of that line when I reflect on his job there. Back in city hall again after fifteen years, my father would have to let someone else try or trumpet certain cases and causes. I think he did it for us. "I got two kids I got late in life. I've got to educate them," were his words to Mr. Chambers the year before. He needed a paycheck to augment his legal fees so he could provide us with everything we needed and all of the extras—first-rate educations (including graduate school) and European study abroad for both David and me. He did a great job at the board, lauded by aldermen for the innovations he brought and the way he crafted language to get bills passed, especially anything that would help black St. Louisans. And he loved working there.

One of my favorite stories about Jordan Chambers arose from Daddy's having worked at the board. My father told it, not only to testify to Chambers's political acumen but also to have a good laugh at himself. Board of Alderman president Alfonso J. Cervantes had mayoral aspirations long before he won the position in 1965. He would discuss them with my father and even told him that, if he were elected, he wanted my dad to be his city counselor. When Daddy, in all seriousness and with a degree of pride, told Jordan, he eyed my dad, paused for an instant, and said, "And you believed him?" My father used to roar out Jordan's line and then laugh so hard that a droplet or two would stream down his face.

My father accepted the position because he would be better able to discharge his responsibility to us, but it took its toll on him. As the years passed, times changed. He still believed in the power of the law and was dismayed to watch violence and riots and irrational ranting sweep through black communities. We had come a long way since "there was no place for us to go in St. Louis," but we had a long way to go. For him, the legal road was still the one best traveled.

He continued laboring within the Democratic Party. In 1960 he served with Eleanor Roosevelt on the National Democratic Platform Committee and helped write the civil rights plank for the Kennedy-Johnson campaign. The following year, he was appointed as a member of the Missouri State Advisory Committee to the U.S. Commission on Civil Rights. And the year after, President Kennedy selected him as a member of the U.S. delegation to Uganda's Uhuru gala when it celebrated its independence from Great Britain. President Johnson also appointed him to his Committee on Government Employment Policy and invited my parents to dinner at the White House.

In spite of these distinctions, I still felt a growing wistfulness within him as he watched my brother throw himself into creative writing and saw my love for art history grow. The realization that he would be unable to pass on his legal expertise and political know-how to one of his children left him wanting. He gave selflessly of his time and diminishing energy to all those who asked for it. Young lawyers, now older and established, who had sought him out still talk about how much they learned from him, how much his very stature and those of his colleagues inspired them to carry on and become the best at their profession. And he still fought battles for respect as a black man, no matter how small. I once accompanied him to the bank we used on Grand Avenue in the late 1970s. When a twenty-something clerk addressed my father as Dave, Daddy roared, "I am old enough to be your grandfather. Don't you EVER call me by my first name again, you hear?"

He may not have fully understood that my brother and I both carried out his legacy in our own ways, not through the law but as public servants. I became a cultural attaché in the U.S. Foreign Service and served my country on four continents as one of a small cadre of black women. My brother ultimately became involved in international conflict resolution, using the methodology of nonviolent action, just as our father had. Throughout our lives, we tried our best to stand up for what we believed in, as did my father, with my mother supporting him in the background.

One story that never got passed around and that bears this out was one only I knew. I had one chance to tell a tale on him to a roomful of his cronies, but didn't. In 1976, a group of St. Louisans formed a committee to celebrate my father's fifty years of service to the community. My mother had initiated it with a call to Ted McNeal, who immediately agreed to handle it. The speakers told story after story of Daddy's courage, intelligence, and honesty and applauded others with whom he had collaborated. One speaker even revealed my father as a "swinger," adding that, "as he matured, his battling became constructive combat."[1] One of the aldermen related how central my dad had been in getting a public accommodations bill passed for the city, which I didn't know. He made sure it was NOT called a civil rights bill since some aldermen would "inwardly flinch at the term" but "they might ask what was meant by a Public Accommodations Bill. The answer of course, was that it was meant to make public places accommodate the public. To this the questioner might respond, 'Don't they do that now?' thus opening the floodgates for exposing all of the mean and petty discriminations of Jim Crow." Daddy wisely added every nationality and nation he could think of "to insure [sic] that such person if he be English, Irish, French, Italian, Spanish, German, Hungarian, Austrian, Slav, Czech, Greek, Lithuanian, Armenian, Russian, Norwegian, Swedish, Polish, Syrian, African, Indian, Chinese, Japanese, Filipino, Etc., not be discriminated against in places of public accommodations."[2]

---

[1] "A Testimonial Honouring David Marshall Grant for His Fifty Years of Distinguished Service as Attorney-at-Law, Public Official and Citizen" (program, St. Louis, September 7, 1975).
[2] Ibid.

David M. Grant's testimonial. Left to right: Grant; publisher of the St. Louis American *newspaper, Nathaniel Sweets; State Senator John Bass; Congressman James Symington; and Bruce Watkins.*

My father threw an imaginary bouquet toward my mother during his response to the well-wishers. He called it a "public acknowledgement and appreciation . . . for her basic understanding and constant support over the years, some of which have been difficult and trying."[3] It was a fine night for him . . . and for her.

---

[3] Ibid.

I just wish I'd had the presence of mind to put myself on the program and give my parents a story about themselves. I know my father could have used it and embellished it better than I could. I didn't do it that evening, but now I can.

By the fall of 1968, college students throughout the United States were outraged by the Vietnam War; university investments in South Africa; and recruitment on college campuses by the CIA and by firms such as Dow Chemical. In addition, black student grievances centered on a lack of course materials recognizing blacks' contributions to U.S. history and society, low minority student enrollment, miniscule financial aid, and campus police harassment. I was a sophomore at Washington University in St. Louis, and we blacks had formed a student union and presented our demands to the university administration, who largely ignored what we wanted. In December 1968, a campus cop roughed up a black law student without cause and, frustrated over the authorities' indifference, we took over the university's administrative office. Or should I say, almost every black student on campus that day did. I was home with the flu and as I watched the news, my temperature went down, my head cleared up, and by the next day, I was sitting in with them. As soon as I arrived, my friends wanted to know if my father would represent us. Daddy said he would come and speak to us.

By the time he showed up, one of the university deans had already asked him to persuade us to leave the premises, promising that the school would begin a dialogue with us. We were costing the university $100,000 per day, and the administration wanted us off of the property. No one believed the administration would keep its word. Daddy accepted our position and agreed to represent us. Then my father said, "All right, now, Gail. You're coming home with me." I just stood there. I didn't say anything. From my silence and the look in my eyes, he knew I wouldn't be going with him. And from the way he gazed at me, I knew he wouldn't, he couldn't, say anything else to me. He turned and left, and I noticed an ever-so-slight droop in his shoulders. He'd lost this one with me. His wanting me home, safe and sound, sprang from his love for me as a father, but he knew he couldn't undermine so much of what he had taught us by forcing me to come with him. "Get a cause!" "Don't back down!" My mother didn't want me there either; they were both worried that violence might erupt, as it had on other campuses. Yet she brought bags of groceries to all of us without exchanging many words with me.

After ten days of occupying the quarters, we straightened up the offices to near perfection and left. There was an official hearing, chaired by a law professor from Harvard. My father represented us without taking a fee, and the university engaged a high-priced, downtown law firm. I had seen campus cops bullying black students since I enrolled, so my father put me in the witness box. He asked me my name and where I lived. "You live there with me, do you?" he asked me in all seriousness. I covered my face with my hand, blushed, and said, "Yes, I do." The room roared with laughter and Daddy chuckled. I had learned a bit about grandstanding from him—how to manipulate an audience or at least how to get its attention. The hearing went well, and it was clear that the university needed to further investigate its police force and to listen to its students.

Thereafter, the university made a real effort to address our ten "demands," one after the other. The journalists were everywhere trying to interview Daddy during the proceedings, and I could feel he was thrilled to be back in the fray, giving counsel to civil rights activists two generations removed from him.

13.

BRINGING IT ALL HOME

*I*FINISHED UNDERGRADUATE SCHOOL AT WASHINGTON University, fulfilling my father's wish that at least one of his children graduate from there. I spent my junior year studying art history in Italy, which would define my future in more ways than I could ever have imagined. The freedom and acceptance I felt there were overwhelming. After finishing graduate school, working at the Smithsonian Institution, and teaching art and architectural history at Howard University for several years, I decided to follow a passion that had been gnawing at me since my year abroad. The thrill of international travel and being able to bond with people from around the world entered my bloodstream while in Europe, and nothing I did could eclipse the rush I got from those memories. I needed to get "on the road" again, so I applied to and was accepted by the Foreign Service. As a cultural attaché, I linked my background in the arts with what was already in my veins. Even my mother, who had acquainted us with the "road" early on, used to say that she never dreamed both my brother and I would take her love of adventure to such lengths. My brother would go to the

Philippines as a Peace Corps volunteer, live in the Netherlands while working for the International Fellowship of Reconciliation, and travel to hot spots on behalf of the Nonviolent Peaceforce, a nongovernmental organization developing the concept and practice of unarmed civilian peacekeeping.

Most people believe that being a diplomat is a glamorous profession. I had my share of that (I met a lot of interesting and famous people and was witness to some history-making events). However, it is a twenty-four-hour-a-day grind because, among other things, you represent the U.S. government at all times while abroad. No matter how much that is drilled into you during your training, no one can prepare you for the reality of what it feels like once you are overseas. Furthermore, there is the danger factor. I entered the service in 1980, while the Iranians were still holding U.S. diplomats in Tehran and random terrorism was on the rise elsewhere. Two years later, after my first overseas posting in Oslo, Norway, I received word that my next job would be in Paris as an assistant cultural attaché. Colonel Charles Ray, a defense attaché, had been killed in Paris exiting his apartment house a few months before I got my "plum" assignment, so I went with a certain amount of trepidation. My parents were terrified. Upon arrival, I was given a standard briefing about the embassy in Paris. "We aren't going to tell the employees the level of alert we are under each day. Just know that we get at least several serious threats every day," I was advised. Furthermore, the security officer told me to vary my route and the time I arrived at the office as much as I could.

For the most part, the Foreign Service is filled with hardworking people who try to keep their chins up and their heads down while they carry out policies with which they don't always personally agree. In addition, friends and family members in the States get married, or have children, or plan reunions, or get ill and die. There is no way a Foreign Service officer can attend many of these passages. I know the anguish it can cause. My father died while I was in Paris. The City of Light is also often cloudy. On that day, it was blindingly sunny, except for a vacant place against the sun that I felt, as I walked to my apartment to pack my things and go home. That morning, he'd died at home with my mother, brother, sister-in-law, and four-month-old niece beside him. That same day, a family friend had represented my father when he was awarded the Black Elks' highest distinction, the Lovejoy Award. Whenever I return to Paris, its wonderment is always overshadowed by these pungent memories.

David M. Grant giving counsel as director of legislative research for the Board of Aldermen, ca. 1980.

All in all, however, my diplomatic career was a good experience for me. I learned a lot, including two more foreign languages, and traveled extensively on four continents. It gave me the feeling that I could go just about anywhere and manage—living in south St. Louis, I feel, also groomed me for my work. And just as I decided to retire (happily and still in one piece), hang up my traveling spurs, and settle in Washington, D.C., the fates took over and I became reacquainted with an Italian man living in Rome whom I had known many years before. The timing wasn't right then, but it was when we saw each other again by chance, and I returned to live in Italy.

I visited St. Louis a few times toward the end of my diplomatic career and once after I moved to Rome. In a certain way, my neighborhood hadn't changed much. Red brick still predominated, and the streets were fairly clean. Stillness hung in the air and permeated the buildings and alleyways, just as it seemed to do when I was a child. There were a few boarded-up buildings I'd never seen, and the candy store looked more like a fortress, its façade almost completely obliterated by tin siding. But there was one glaring difference—the people who lived there were different.

In a locale that was once as segregated as any in 1950s America, I now saw blacks and whites, Asians, Africans, West Indians, and Middle Easterners, plus a solid contingent of Bosnians, living side by side. When I visited Sam's Shoe Repair and greeted the proprietors, I thanked them for their kindness and broached their lack of prejudice, a subject we had never discussed until then. Mrs. "Sam," who still maintained her flaming red hair after more than forty years, answered, "Yes, you were among the first who made a mark down here. Things have opened up a lot since then. And your family started it."

On my next visit to St. Louis, I learned they had closed their shop for good shortly after I had last seen them. I was saddened not to know where they had gone or not to have been able to say good-bye. But at least I had finally expressed my gratitude for the haven they had offered me.

On one Christmas visit, my mother and I attended Midnight Mass at St. Pius V Church, before the elementary school closed its doors. The atmosphere could not have been more different from when I used to process into a darkened church packed with parishioners. At the stroke of midnight, holding a lighted candle and wearing a white gown and a handkerchief-like veil bobby-pinned in my hair, I would arrive with the girls' choir and march down the aisle singing Christmas carols. Now, Mass started at 10:30 p.m. with every electric bulb switched on inside the barely half-full nave. The dozen or so candles on the altar lost their magic in the brightness. The only procession came midway through when a Vietnamese and a Ghanaian child, dressed in their national garb, presented the wine and bread to the priest for consecration. An Eastern European boy read one of the lessons and a Thai child another.

I was astonished by what I saw, never dreaming that there would be such an ethnic mix under the same roof in south St. Louis. During Mass, I reflected on all of the years I had spent in this neighborhood, in this church and its school, and I mulled over some of the experiences I'd had. How much time I had spent in prayer here, or in confession, or excitedly scurrying to church for the May Day procession with a wreath of spring flowers, even if artificial, on my head. How my first-grade school nun favored me—at least I thought she did from her warm embraces and constant encouragement. How, as a teenager, I smarted when a grown woman bolted from her seat as I sat down next to her for

Mass and almost tripped as she jumped over my feet and rushed away for a bench as far away from me as possible. But also how a slightly older boy I knew from grade school had left his pew to take her place beside me when he saw what happened. And how I stopped regularly attending Sunday Mass after that incident. How many times I had awakened at dawn to walk the nine, interminable blocks so I could direct the girls' choir at the 8:00 a.m. daily Requiem Mass. After all, out of all of the eighth graders, the nuns had chosen me to lead the choir. And how many times on my way to and from school I had passed a house where another colored family lived. And how they were never able, no matter how ferociously they scrubbed the side of their home, to erase fully the word "NIGGER," painted there in thick, white letters by some anonymous passerby. How many times a faceless somebody in a speeding car had called me a nigger. How many times I did not walk down the aisle as part of a friend's wedding party; their parents just wouldn't allow it. But then again, how one of my girlfriends refused to be her best friend's maid of honor because I wasn't invited to be a bridesmaid. The good and the bad all balled up together. I finally put this confusing part of my life behind me. There was nothing here that could harm me anymore.

And then I thought about what my life would have been like if I had remained at All Saints Episcopal Church, located down the street and around the corner from where my mother had grown up, and where my father had been an altar boy, and where my great uncles had sung in the men's choir. A church I remember for its cordiality—a church where everyone knew my name even before I did, and where I went to Sunday school until I started first grade and began attending Catholic Mass every day. What if I had stayed at Miss Stallworth's Dance Academy on the north side with all of the other preschool colored girls for tap and ballet lessons? What if I'd joined the Jack and Jill social club and been sought after for my looks? And what if I had found my charming knight and brought him home to a new, worldlier St. Louis after visiting faraway places with strange-sounding names, which was the other part of my wish? What if?

As Mother and I left Mass and greeted the pastor in the vestibule, I told him that my brother and I had integrated the school many years earlier. Moreover, I said that we had been the only blacks there from 1950, when my brother entered, until 1963 when I graduated. He reacted by hiking his shoulders and appearing as if I had just backed him up against a wall:

"Things are just fine now. Well, of course, we have some difficulties but everything is fine, just fine."

All I really expected from him was a question, maybe, about what it was like to break the color line at the school. But from his body language and the elevated pitch of his voice, it was evident that "things" were not as relatively peaceful in south St. Louis as they seemed to me. That night, however, I was glad to take what I saw at face value.

I also reflected on how much of my life had been defined by my race. Where I went to school (elementary through college), what religion I chose, my yearning to go somewhere else and be free of labels and stereotypes, even how I drank my coffee and tea. I only learned the reason behind this habit a few years ago. It would be the last story my mother told me and the only one I'd never heard growing up: why we had only cups and saucers in our house and never mugs.

By the time she told it to me, I was finally living in a condo in Washington, D.C., large and comfortable enough to have houseguests. It seemed as if within a space of a month, two of my best girlfriends visited and both remarked about my lack of mugs.

They both liked to drink larger amounts of tea or coffee than my dainty teacups could hold. "I'll have to send you some as a house-warming gift," they both said. As mugs became more popular as keepsakes from weekend getaways or summer destinations in the 1970s, my mother did garner a small collection, but they were usually received as gifts from friends and we rarely used them. The next time I saw her, then living about a mile from me in D.C., we talked about this custom.

"We never had them at 2620 because of the racetrack, so I never wanted them either," came her nonsensical reply. She then explained that Grandma loved going to the races, especially at the dog track across the river in Illinois. Nathaniel, of course, would drive and accompany her onto the grounds. I knew about Grandma fancying the track but nothing more than that. Anyone, black or white, could bet. My grandmother never intentionally passed for white but if someone made the mistake, she usually said nothing. It was like a secret joke she could pull on white people for an hour or so. When she saw that Negroes received their beverages only in heavy mugs with thick handles while whites received their drinks in cups and saucers, she was livid. She pushed her saucer and tea-cup aside and thereafter went thirsty at the track. From then on, everyone at 2620 was served with a cup and saucer. My mother never brought mugs into our house, and I, by rote, did the same.

On my last visit home, I happened to be in town for the official announcement of an endowed chair named for Marga-ret Bush Wilson at Washington University. Margaret was still practicing law and fighting for racial equality. Most of the black bourgeoisie were present. My parents' friends and some of their children had come out to support Margaret and applaud the university's pricey acknowledgment of her contribution to the community and the country. My father had given Margaret her first job out of law school, and she had kindly seated me up front. Several other up-front attendees quizzically looked at me and I heard a few voices from behind me, asking who I was. I had to tilt my name tag and point to it before they recognized me. It had been a long time. Nonetheless, they all knew my story. How I had moved to Rome and would soon be marrying an Italian. My mother, now living in Washington, often spoke with her friends,

Left to right: Judge Anne Marie Clarke, Judge Donald McCullin, Margaret Bush Wilson, her son Robert Wilson III, Mary Clarke, and Gail Milissa Grant in 2005.

and word had spread throughout the community. And they were all thrilled for me. I imagined some of their commentary:

"She certainly took after her mother, all that traveling."

"She comes from such a good stock. I'm so happy that she's finally getting married. I wonder what took her so long."

"And living in Rome, married to an Italian man. My word. How romantic."

In spite of their well wishes, it was somewhat unsettling to be almost anonymous amongst the people whom I had admired and who had served as my role models. I had paid a price that, however eager I was to pay, still left me feeling detached from my roots.

Dr. John Baugh, the professor who would hold Margaret's chair, spoke of something that made me feel a bit more connected. That day marked the thirty-seventh anniversary of the day the Association of Black Collegians, myself included, then occupying part of the university's administration building, had presented the authorities with a list of ten demands. And the university, over the years, had addressed every one of them.

Above all, I fulfilled my parents' weightiest mandate. I got stronger. They walked their talk and by so doing, I felt I could establish and walk my own. I fully realized just how much being a black person had lifted me out of everydayness and placed me on a world stage—how much strength and wisdom I had received from all those at whose elbows I sat and in whose footsteps I'd followed. And how I owed it all to my parents, even though I had complained about where we lived, who my friends were, and how I had wanted to belong to the colored side of town.

And I got my childhood wishes and then some. I lived and worked on three continents with plenty of people who looked like me, and I traveled to even more. America was reluctant to appreciate my brand of beauty, but finally it caught up with Italy, and I was considered good-looking almost wherever I went. And I got my knight, who had become a king by now. And I then came home to say good-bye and move on.

"And that's the way she goes."

Credo of the American Negro Citizen a.d. 1942

Credo Committee

David M. Grant, Chairman

Saint Louis Branch, NAACP

I am an American Citizen

My countrymen call me 'Negro.'

But no matter what I am called, the fact remains that I am a citizen of the United States of American, native born.

As such, I expect to share ALL the responsibilities and obligations of Good Citizenship.

I HAVE shared these obligations and responsibilities.

My record bears proof abundant.

My Crispus Attucks died first on Boston Commons for my country's freedom in 1770.

My Robert Brooks died first in the Philippines for my country's democracy in 1941.

But I have NOT shared the opportunities and rewards of Good Citizenship.

WITNESS:

My government allows nine millions of me to be denied the right to vote for the very sheriff who may stand between me and the mob that would lynch me.

My government allows me to be segregated in slum ghettos.

I am shoved around and doled out the crumbs from the employment host and boss, and told where to sit, if at all, in dining rooms my government operates.

There is no room for gainful employment of me in my government's civilian defense program, and my volunteer efforts, I am told, are to be rewarded with picks, shovels, and tar brooms on demolition street gangs.

My government winks at my degradations and expects my soul-sickness to be cured by hired "representatives" and fruitless investigations.

My government is soul-sick, too, but it is not aware of this as I am; and when I think of proud France, that was soul-sick also and not aware, I shudder and grow afraid for my government.

My government is in distress, and it expects me to help—and I will help; fully, gladly and patriotically will

I pledge allegiance to the American Flag and to the Republic for which it stands; one nation, indivisible with Liberty and Justice for all—

But despite my national patriotism as an American citizen, I cannot freely render my full measure of loyal aid,

SO LONG AS

I can enlist in my government's navy as mess attendant only,

SO LONG AS

I am barred completely from my government's marine corps,

SO LONG AS

I am hired only as porter or menial in my government's defense plants and denied my station on the production line,

SO LONG AS

I am forbidden to fly the mighty ships of my government's Navy of the Skies.

Let me die in combat with my government's army as a free soldier, and not a segregated one.

And when peace is come again, let my government be honorable and forthright about me—For too well do I remember the quarter century of 1917 to 1942.

My government is strong and I am weak.

My government must defend me, for I am defenseless.

My government must protect me for I am unprotected.

Let my government BE the democracy she PROCLAIMS.

I am the test of my government.

I am the test of my country's integrity of soul, her honesty of purpose.

I am the TEST of DEMOCRACY.

BIBLIOGRAPHY

Allen, Michael R. "A Short History of Homer G. Phillips Hospital." Ecology of Absence, 2005. www.eco-absence.org/stl/hgp/history. htm.

Baker, Jean-Claude, and Chris Chase. *Josephine: The Hungry Heart.* New York: Random House, 1993.

Baker, Josephine, speech at Kiel Opera House, February 3, 1952. University of Missouri–St. Louis Black History Project (1980–1983). Western Historical Manuscript Collection, UMSL.

Capeci, Dominic, Jr. *The Lynching of Cleo Wright.* Lexington: University Press of Kentucky, 1998.

"Early History of Nursing Schools in St. Louis, The." Bernard Becker Medical Library Digital Collection, 2004. http://beckerexhibits. wustl.edu/mowihsp/health/stlnursingschools.htm.

Elks News 64, no. 1 (July 1985).

Employee's Loan Company. *Negroes: Their Gift to St. Louis.* St. Louis: Author, 1964.

Federal Bureau of Investigation. David Grant, main file no. 100-231059.

"Fighting for Democracy in St. Louis: Civil Rights During World War II." *Missouri Historical Review* LXXX, no. 1 (October, 1985): 58–75.

Freeman, Frankie Muse, with Candace O'Connor. *A Song of Faith and Hope: The Life of Frankie Muse Freeman.* St. Louis: Missouri Historical Society Press, 2003.

Graham, Jamie R., with research by Girl Friends, Inc., of St. Louis. *Shelley vs. Kraemer: A Celebration.* St. Louis: The Chapter, 1988.

Haney, Lynn. *Naked at the Feast: A Biography of Josephine Baker.* New York: Dodd, Mead, 1981.

Heathcott, Joseph. "Black Archipelago: Politics and Civic Life in the Jim Crow City." *Journal of Social History* (Spring 2005).

Hinton, Curtis L. *You Can't Arrest Freedom* (documentary on the St. Louis Civil Rights movement), 1995.

Garreau, Joel. *The Nine Nations of North America.* Boston: Houghton Mifflin, 1981.

Grant, Louise Elizabeth. "The Saint Louis Unit of the March on Washington: A Study in the Sociology of Conflict." Ph.D. diss., Fisk University, 1944.

Oral History Project, Black Leaders, Western Historical Manuscript Collection. www.umsl.edu.

Organ, Claude H., Jr., and Margaret M. Kosiba, eds. *A Century of Black Surgeons.* Norman, OK: Transcript Press, 1987.

Pickard, Elizabeth A. "Opening the Gates: Segregation, Desegregation, and the Story of Lewis Place." *Gateway* 26, no. 2 (Fall 2005).

Welek, Mary. "Jordan Chambers: Black Politician and Boss." *The Journal of Negro History* LVII (October 4, 1972).

Young, F. Weldon. *The '30s, Donnybrook Decade in St. Louis Public School Power Plants: A Geechee Mavericks Quest in a Jim Crow City.* St. Louis: Nathan B. Young Historic Memorial, 1984.

Young, N. B. *Your St. Louis and Mine.* St. Louis: Author, 1937.

INTERVIEWS WITH:

Boon, Ina

Bynum, Marsha

Carper, George

Duckett, Leola Amoureaux

Dugas, June

Elliott, Forriss

Freeman, Frankie

Grant, David W.

Grant, Mildred

McMillian, Theodore

McNeal, Virgie

Rodgers, Benny

Roxborough, Mildred

Saunders, Ann Camille

Sweets, Ellen

Symington, James W.

Wilson, Margaret Bush

Young, Ira

Index

01/27/09